Grinnell College

Grinnell, Iowa

Written by Lauren Standifer
Edited by Kevin Nash and Adam Burns

Additional contributions by Omid Gohari,
Christina Koshzow, Chris Mason, Joey Rahimi, Jon Skindzier,
Luke Skurman, Tim Williams, and Kimberly Moore

ISBN # 1-59658-056-9
ISSN # 1551-0161
© Copyright 2005 College Prowler
All Rights Reserved
Printed in the U.S.A.
www.collegeprowler.com

Special thanks to Babs Carryer, Andy Hannah, LaunchCyte, Tim O'Brien, Bob Sehlinger, Thomas Emerson, Andrew Skurman, Barbara Skurman, Bert Mann, Dave Lehman, Daniel Fayock, Chris Babyak, The Donald H. Jones Center for Entrepreneurship, Terry Slease, Jerry McGinnis, Bill Ecenberger, Idie McGinty, Kyle Russell, Jacque Zaremba, Larry Winderbaum, Paul Kelly, Roland Allen, Jon Reider, Team Evankovich, Julie Fenstermaker, Lauren Varacalli, Abu Noaman, Jason Putorti, Mark Exler, Daniel Steinmeyer, Jared Cohon, Gabriela Oates, Tri Ad Litho, David Koegler, Glen Meakem, and the Grinnell Bounce Back Team.

College Prowler™
5001 Baum Blvd.
Suite 456
Pittsburgh, PA 15213

Phone: (412) 697-1390, 1(800) 290-2682
Fax: (412) 697-1396, 1(800) 772-4972
E-mail: info@collegeprowler.com
Website: www.collegeprowler.com

College Prowler™ is not sponsored by, affiliated with, or approved by Grinnell College in any way.

College Prowler™ strives faithfully to record its sources. As the reader understands, opinions, impressions, and experiences are necessarily personal and unique. Accordingly, there are, and can be, no guarantees of future satisfaction extended to the reader.

© Copyright 2005 College Prowler. All rights reserved. No part of this work may be reproduced or transmitted in any form or by any means, including but not limited to, photocopy, recording, or any information storage and retrieval systems, without the express written permission of College Prowler™.

Welcome to College Prowler™

During the writing of College Prowler's guidebooks, we felt it was critical that our content was unbiased and unaffiliated with any college or university. We think it's important that our readers get honest information and a realistic impression of the student opinions on any campus — that's why if any aspect of a particular school is terrible, we (unlike a campus brochure) intend to publish it. While we do keep an eye out for the occasional extremist — the cheerleader or the cynic — we take pride in letting the students tell it like it is. We strive to create a book that's as representative as possible of each particular campus. Our books cover both the good and the bad, and whether the survey responses point to recurring trends or a variation in opinion, these sentiments are directly and proportionally expressed through our guides.

College Prowler guidebooks are in the hands of students throughout the entire process of their creation. Because you can't make student-written guides without the students, we have students at each campus who help write, randomly survey their peers, edit, layout, and perform accuracy checks on every book that we publish. From the very beginning, student writers gather the most up-to-date stats, facts, and inside information on their colleges. They fill each section with student quotes and summarize the findings in editorial reviews. In addition, each school receives a collection of letter grades (A through F) that reflect student opinion and help to represent contentment, prominence, or satisfaction for each of our 20 specific categories. Just as in grade school, the higher the mark the more content, more prominent, or more satisfied the students are with the particular category.

Once a book is written, additional students serve as editors and check for accuracy even more extensively. Our bounce-back team — a group of randomly selected students who have no involvement with the project — are asked to read over the material in order to help ensure that the book accurately expresses every aspect of the university and its students. This same process is applied to the 200-plus schools College Prowler currently covers. Each book is the result of endless student contributions, hundreds of pages of research and writing, and countless hours of hard work. All of this has led to the creation of a student information network that stretches across the nation to every school that we cover. It's no easy accomplishment, but it's the reason that our guides are such a great resource.

When reading our books and looking at our grades, keep in mind that every college is different and that the students who make up each school are not uniform — as a result, it is important to assess schools on a case-by-case basis. Because it's impossible to summarize an entire school with a single number or description, each book provides a dialogue, not a decision, that's made up of 20 different topics and hundreds of student quotes. In the end, we hope that this guide will serve as a valuable tool in your college selection process. Enjoy!

OMID GOHARI ○ CHRISTINA KOSHZOW ○ CHRIS MASON ○ JOEY RAHIMI ○ LUKE SKURMAN ○
The College Prowler™ Team

GRINNELL COLLEGE
Table of Contents

By the Numbers............................ **1**	Campus Strictness..................... **93**
Academics **4**	Parking... **97**
Local Atmosphere **10**	Transportation **102**
Safety and Security................... **18**	Weather.................................... **107**
Computers.................................. **22**	Report Card Summary **112**
Facilities...................................... **27**	Overall Experience **113**
Campus Dining.......................... **32**	The Inside Scoop.................... **116**
Off-Campus Dining **40**	Finding a Job or Internship **122**
Campus Housing....................... **47**	Alumni Information................. **124**
Off-Campus Housing................ **57**	Student Organizations............ **126**
Diversity..................................... **62**	The Best & Worst.................... **131**
Guys and Girls **69**	Visiting Campus...................... **133**
Athletics..................................... **76**	Words to Know....................... **137**
Nightlife..................................... **82**	
Drug Scene............................... **88**	

Introduction from the Author

When you tell people you go to Grinnell College in Iowa, a common response is "Oh, Cornell? I heard that's a really good school." Or, "Grinnell, isn't that just west of The University of Iowa?' Have you ever been to a Hawkeye's football game!?'" In other words, very few people have actually heard of Grinnell, and those who have heard of it usually associate the school with its close proximity to the University of Iowa or, more precisely, Iowa's football team, the state's crown jewel. Despite its stellar academics, its national recognition in ESPN the Magazine, and (allegedly) in Playboy's overall student attractiveness rankings, and despite the fact that many students at Grinnell view their school as the best place a college student could ever hope to be. Grinnell remains an outright mystery. Many students, however, are quite content with the school's ambiguity.

Sometimes, living smack dab in the middle of an endless plain of cornfields can feel a little confining, and occasionally students feel like they're living in a soundproof bubble where news from the outside world trickles in only occasionally. Of course, in the world we live in today this is not altogether a bad thing. Grinnell then, in a sense, is a bit like Thomas Moore's Utopia, an ideal sanctuary on a tiny remote island in the middle of an ocean of, well, farmland. Here, it's easy to forget that somewhere in the world, there is bigotry and random violence. Yeah, the troubles of the world seem non-existent in a town that hasn't had a murder since the Nixon administration.

At the same time, most Grinnell students consider themselves just as active, attentive, and up-to-date on world events here as they would be in the heart of Manhattan. Students here can express their feelings about issues, such as the war in Iraq and gay rights, without ever having to worry about being condemned by an overly-conservative hierarchy. Yes, we have a very liberal student body. This is due in large part to the Grinnell professors, who constantly encourage their students to push their intellectual limits and think about the world in a new light. "Grinnellians" are constantly inundated by new and fascinating ideas that they just wouldn't get on television or the Internet.

Of course, everything isn't all "peaches and cream" at Grinnell (go to school in Georgia if you want peaches). Complaints about the food, the workload, and the social claustrophobia of the surrounding town are not uncommon, and life in Iowo takes a little getting used to if you are from out-of-state. However, the fact remains that most students who choose to stay here will tell you that the top-notch academics that you'll receive, and the lifelong friendships that you'll most likely forge, make spending four years of your life in Iowa well worth it. Maybe you could be one of the chosen few to attend our fine university, or maybe you'd be happier somewhere else, where there's a prestigious business school, a wide variety of five-star restaurants, and a plethora of all-night dance clubs within walking distance. At the very least, it's worth a close look and a visit, because if Grinnell is your kind of school (and this guidebook will help you determine if it is), you shouldn't let anything stand in your way. Well, you bought the book, so that's step 1: Step 2 is reading through it and deciding if Grinnell is for you or not.

Lauren Standifer, Author

By the Numbers

General Information
Grinnell College
1210 Park St
Grinnell, Iowa 50112

Control:
Private

Academic Calendar:
Semester

Religious Affiliation:
None

Founded:
1846

Website:
http://www.grinnell.edu

Main Phone:
641-269-4000

Admissions Phone:
800-247-0113

Student Body

Full-Time Undergraduates:
1,485

Part-Time Undergraduates:
39

Full-Time Males:
686

Full-Time Females:
838

Male to Female Ratio:
45% to 55%

Admissions

Overall Acceptance Rate: 63%

Early Decision Acceptance Rate: 79%

Regular Decision Acceptance Rate: 62%

Total Applicants: 2,284

Total Acceptances: 1,443

Freshman Enrollment: 405

Yield (% of admitted students who actually enroll): 28.1%

Applicants Placed on Waiting List: 244

Applicants Accepted From Waiting List: 93

Students Enrolled From Waiting List: 1

Transfer Applications Received: 126

Transfer Applications Accepted: 39

Transfer Students Enrolled: 13

Transfer Applicant Acceptance Rate: 31%

Early Decision Available? Yes

Early Action Available? No

Early Decision One Deadline: November 20

Early Decision Two Deadline: January 1

Early Decision One Reply Date: January 20

Early Decision Two Reply Date: February 15

Early Decision One Notification: December 20

Early Decision Two Notification: February 1

Regular Decision Deadline: January 20

Regular Decision Notification: April 1

Regular Decision Reply Date: May 1

Common Application Accepted? Yes

Supplemental Forms? Yes

Admissions Phone: 800-247-0113

Admissions E-mail: askgrin@grinnell.edu

Admissions Website: http://www.grinnell.edu/admission

SAT I or ACT Required? Either

First-Year Students Submitting SAT Scores:
82%

SAT I Range (25th – 75th Percentile):
1240 – 1450

SAT I Verbal Range (25th – 75th Percentile):
610 – 730

SAT I Math Range (25th – 75th Percentile):
630 – 720

Retention Rate: 91%

SAT II Requirements:
Math and Writing

First-Year Students Submitting ACT Scores: 54%

ACT Range (25th – 75th Percentile): 28-31

ACT English Range (25th – 75th Percentile): 27-32

ACT Math Range (25th – 75th Percentile): 26-31

Top 10% of High School Class:
62%

Application Fee:
$30

Financial Information

Full-Time Tuition:
$25,820

Room and Board:
$6,870

Books and Supplies for class:
$400 (average for the year)

Average Need-Based Financial Aid Package:
$20,298
(including loans, work-study, grants, and other sources)

Students Who Applied For Financial Aid: 61%

Students Who Received Aid:
60%

Financial Aid Forms Deadline:
February 1

Required Financial Aid Forms:
FAFSA
Noncustodial Parent's Statement
Grinnell's Financial Aid forms

Financial Aid Phone:
800-247-0113 or 641-269-3250

Financial Aid E-mail:
finaid@grinnell.edu

Financial Aid Website:
http://www.grinnell.edu/offices/financialaid

Academics

The Lowdown On...
Academics

Degrees Awarded:
Bachelor's

Most Popular Majors:
11% biology,
9% English and literature,
8% sociology,
7% history,
6% political science

Average Course Load:
Four

Full-Time Faculty:
140

Faculty with Terminal Degree:
95%

Student-to-Faculty Ratio:
9.5:1

4 Year Graduation Rate %:
80%

5 Year Graduation Rate %:
84%

6 Year Graduation Rate %:
85%

Special Degree Options
3-2 Engineering Program, Teacher Certification program

AP Test Score Requirements
Possible credit for scores of 4 or 5

IB Test Score Requirements:
Possible credit for scores of 5 or above on HL exams

Did You Know?

The only required classes you have to take are the Freshman Tutorial and the requirements for your major.

Best Places to Study
Burling Library, Bob's Underground, "The Elbow" in Noyce

Students Speak Out On...
Academics

> "Most of the professors that I've had truly invested themselves in the students and the material. They also had high expectations for their students."

Q "**Most of my teachers have been incredible**, but a few have been really bad. Even at worst, professors are accessible at almost all hours and are competent in their field. At best (and best is often the case) the teachers serve to inspire and create an environment of comprehensive enjoyment for the material outside the classroom. I hated high school, but these classes are great."

Q "The **teachers here are the hardest, most intelligent, most understanding teachers** I've ever had. There are classes that you'll go into knowing that you won't get an A, but you are guaranteed to learn more than you ever have in one class. Teachers who do not push their students often end up having the students push them (figuratively, of course), or push the class themselves. The only class that I have had that was not interesting to me was improved by outside discussions with fellow students."

Q "**Classes are challenging**, but well worth the effort, if you wake up in time to get to them."

Q "Of course my classes are interesting, and one of the wonderful things about my liberal arts education is that **all of my classes seem to interweave and relate to each other**. Some professors here would rather be doing research all of the time, but most are very concerned with the learning that takes place in their classroom."

Q "**The professors at Grinnell are amazing**! They all seem so interested in what they are teaching. My classes have all been really fun and interesting."

Q "The teachers are, for the most part, quite good. There are a couple classes that, although I have no interest in, I would take just because of the teacher. The **teachers know their stuff and are open-minded** about classroom ideas."

Q "Your **academic experience here depends entirely on the department you choose**. They are all very willing to have one-on-one interactions with students; they enjoy their subject, and they are genuinely interested in helping you in whatever way they can."

Q "Professors are very accessible and are willing to help any student who comes to see them. They are engaging in class, and are very informative. The **professors are concerned not only about a student's performance in class, but their general well being in life**. The classes are generally quite interesting. There are some classes that aren't as good as others (i.e. statistics), but most classes are interesting and fun."

Q "**There aren't a lot of options in the course catalog**, which is one disadvantage of having a small school. Luckily though, the few classes that are available have excellent professors who know what they're talking about and, generally, are more than happy to devote individual attention after class. It's also usually a good idea to stay away from temporary Profs. Fortunately they are few and far between."

Q "Most of the classes for my major (Sociology) were interesting. The professors tried their best to make the class time go by fast. Most Profs are older men who have a lot of experience in their field. We are **starting to get more minorities and women professors**, which is a good thing."

The College Prowler Take On...
Academics

The pride and joy of Grinnell College is, and always has been, its academic reputation. When our football team loses time after time, when it's negative eleven degrees outside, when potheads smell up the social lounges, and when yet another giant pit has replaced an outdated building; Grinnellian's can always fall back on the great education they're receiving. Most of the classes at Grinnell are extremely challenging and, when all is said and done, very rewarding as well. Most professors constantly challenge their students to think critically and demand a lot, in terms of quality work. Anything a professor assigns is aimed at helping the student understand what they're studying, rather than just passing on another deadline. Normally, few classes give out excessive homework, but this doesn't mean that courses here are easy. It simply means that professors expect the few papers that you do turn in to be well thought out and well written. In the humanities and social studies departments, professors assign much reading, and (get this) actually expect the students to do it!

The fact that most of the students who come to Grinnell are intelligent does not necessarily mean that everyone does well. The atmosphere is not competitive, and bad grades are common. Students who consistently make below a C average are put on academic probation and can be subject to expulsion, but there are some students who have been on probation for most of their Grinnell career and are still around. In terms of required courses, Grinnell is pretty lax. The only course required for all students is the Freshman Tutorial, which is a writing class that focuses on an interesting topic like "Utopia and Revolution in Russia and the US", "Stealing Home, Killing Time; A Cultural Study of Baseball" or, "Frankenstein: Gender, Technology, and the Sociological Imagination." If these courses don't tickle your intellectual fancy, then I don't know what will? Your tutorial professor is automatically your adviser until you declare a major, so choose wisely, and check out the website www.ratemyprofessor.com beforehand.

The College Prowler™ Grade on
Academics: B+

A high Academics grade generally indicates that professors are knowledgeable, accessible, and genuinely interested in their students' welfare. Other determining factors include class size, how well professors communicate, and whether or not classes are engaging.

Local Atmosphere

The Lowdown On...
Local Atmosphere

Region:
Midwest

City, State:
Grinnell, Iowa

Setting:
Small town

Distance from Des Moines:
1 hours

Distance from Iowa City:
1 hours

Points of Interest:
Rocj Creek State Park
Covrell's Pumpkin Farm
Community Art Galleries downtown
Dari Barn

Closest Amusement Park:

Adventure Land
I-80 and Highway 65
Des Moines, Iowa
515-266-2121

Closest Shopping Malls or Plazas:

Coral RidgeMall
Highway 965 & I-80
Coralville IA

Marshall Town Center
US Rt 30 & Iowa Rt 14
Marshalltown, IA

Closest Movie Theaters:

Capitol Theater
116 1st Avenue East
Newton, IA 50208
Phone: 641-792-1862

Newton Community Theaters
1701 South 8th Avenue East
Newton, IA 50208
Phone: 641-792-1230

Valle Drive In
4074 Highway F 48 West
Newton, IA, 50208
Phone: 641-792-3558

Major Sports Teams:
Iowa Hawkeyes
Iowa State Cyclones
Northern Iowa Panthers
Iowa Barnstormers (football)

City Websites
http://www.grinnelliowa.gov
http://www.grinnelliowa.com

Local Slang:

Pop: That bubbly sweet cola with oh-so-many names.
Townie: A local Grinnell townsperson, usually identified by over-sized under-washed overalls or an early 1970s pick-up truck.

Did You Know?

5 Fun Facts about Iowa:

1. Iowa ranks first in the US in egg, hog, soybean, and corn production.

2. Iowa is home to three state universities, sixty-two public and private colleges, and twenty-eight community colleges

3. Iowa is equidistant from the Atlantic and the Pacific

4. Field of Dreams, Huckleberry Finn, Bridges of Madison County, Starman, Children of the Corn, Twister, Pennies from Heaven, and Zadar: Cow from Hell were all filmed in Iowa. (What! You haven't seen Zadar? You don't know what you're missing!)

5. Surprisingly, Iowa is a big jazz state and hosts the Bix Festival every year in Davenport.

Famous People from Iowa:

John Wayne, Johnny Carson, Tom Arnold, Grant Wood, Grace Pearl Ingalls, Phil Strong, Laura Ingalls Wilder, Elmer and Fred Maytag, John Deere, Abigail Van Buren, Anne Landers, Leon "Bix" Beiderbeck, Glen Miller, Chief Blackhawk, Norman Borlaug, Mamie Eisenhower, Carrie Chapman Catt, Jesse and Frank James, Wyatt and Virgil Earp, William "Buffalo Bill" Cody, The Ringling Brothers, Herbert Hoover, George Washington Carver, Ashton Kutcher

Students Speak Out On...
Local Atmosphere

> "The town is really cute and charming, but the townies resent the presence of the students. There is a great little art shop in town that sells all sorts of cool stuff from awesome candles to antique wind chimes."

Q "**Grinnell is a small one-college town**. Most people in town are very friendly and personable."

Q "Grinnell is in the middle of a cornfield, but that doesn't mean it's not a great place to live. **Iowa City and Des Moines are not very far away**, so if you have a car you shouldn't have a problem finding something to do. The townspeople are friendly and get along well with college students."

Q "I'm a minority and, for me, the atmosphere is fine most of the times. However, on the weekends the townies (especially the teenagers) **make comments both racial and sexual**. I disregard it, though, because they are from Grinnell, Iowa. What do they know?"

Q "Some parts of Grinnell are full of residents **who are inclined to help students in any way they can**. However, there is a section of town where people drive by in their pick-ups and yell profanities out the window, even if you are minding your own business."

Q "The atmosphere is, in one word: **laid-back**."

Q "If I hear another **potato joke** I'm gonna punch somebody in the face!"

Q "Ha! Grinnell has a town population of about 9000 people, so unless you count the community college a half hour away, there are no other universities present. Grinnell is a very friendly rural town that is struggling to survive in an age of hog lots and big business. **There is a very good relationship between the college and the town** because neither one would survive without the benefit of the other. Things to visit in town: Saint's Rest, a local coffee house owned by an alum; the local bakery at 2 a.m., when there are freshly baked goods; any one of the various parks in town; the farmer's market, and music in the park during the summer and fall. Stay away from high school townies though."

Q "The **town resembles a 1950s farm-community**—pretty boring stuff. Most students use downtown for random commerce, the bars, and for daily necessities. However, due to the residency requirement on campus, social isolation isn't a problem; the social scene is great and localized entirely within the campus."

Q "The town of Grinnell is really nice. It is sort of like **a rural slum that has a college plunked down in the middle of it**. There is a huge divide between the people associated with the college, and the humble townsfolk. High school kids will definitely yell stuff at you as you walk down the street, but the downtown has really nice stores that are staffed by friendly, interesting people."

Q "No other colleges are in town, and there really isn't anything to stay away from because **there isn't much to do here**. The town is cute and there is a good relationship between the college and the town. Iowa City and Des Moines aren't too far away if one needs to get out of Grinnell, and the college offers shuttles to these cities for $5 on most weekends. However, the college and students usually provide enough activities. So, there's no reason to leave on the weekends."

Q "**The town is lame**, but there really isn't any need to go anywhere else, (other than the occasional trip to Wal-Mart). Practically everything you need is right on campus. Luckily, it's not too far away from Iowa City, where you can get a change of scenery and decent food. If you don't have a car, I'd find a friend who does."

The College Prowler Take On...
Local Atmosphere

When parents and friends ask students where Grinnell College is located, many respond "In the middle of a corn field." This is simply not true. Prospective students should be informed that we are actually located at the southern end of the field. All kidding aside, a ten-minute walk is all that it takes to reach downtown Grinnell. The setting is, in two words: extremely rural. A number of students feel constricted by the small size of the town. Basically, every store you would want to visit can be found on either Broad St. or Main St, and if you're not sure, you can walk down one end and up the other in about five minutes. Wal-Mart is a five to ten minute drive away from the campus, yet Grinnell is still lacking in a number of amenities that students from urban areas are used to. The campus was thrilled this semester when a second Chinese food restaurant opened, but you still have to drive to Marshalltown to get Mexican cuisine, and, currently, the nearest non-college-owned movie theater is in Newton, which is about twenty minutes away.

Living in a cow town does, however, have some significant perks. Unless you plan on visiting other towns on a regular basis, a car is completely unnecessary. Everything is easily within walking distance and on warm fall or spring nights a casual walk to the local Dari Barn can be really satisfying. The population is small enough that when you go out shopping, you're bound to run into people you know and senseless crime is virtually non-existent. Leaving your car unlocked and knowing that it will be there when you get back is a luxury few people in a big city can claim. Since a good chunk of Grinnell's population, and henceforth a sizable portion of its income, is made up of students, there are a lot of stores that cater specifically to college students' wallets. There are also two trendy coffee shops complete with art for sale in the downtown area. So, while Grinnell isn't very big, there are always things to do. Moreover, the students who stay here either love the small town atmosphere, or learn to deal with it. The students who are driven completely insane by living in the middle of nowhere usually leave after a year or two.

The College Prowler™ Grade on

Local Atmosphere: C

A high Local Atmosphere grade indicates that the area surrounding campus is safe and scenic. Other factors include nearby attractions, proximity to other schools, and the town's attitude toward students

Safety & Security

The Lowdown On...
Safety & Security

Number of Grinnell Security Guards:
10

Public Safety Phone:
641-269-4600

Safety Services:
Escort Service
Self-Defense Classes
Shuttles to airports and hospital

Health Services:
Over the counter medication, dressings and inoculations; HIV and pregnancy testing; offers two free condoms per student per day; walk-in counseling; psychological services; overnight care; and morning-after pills

Health Phone:
641-269-3230

Health Center Office Hours
8:00 a.m. to 5:00 p.m. Monday through Friday

Students Speak Out On...
Safety & Security

> "Dorms are on twenty-four-hour lockdown but, for the most part, security is pretty lax and students don't feel the need to lock their doors."

Q "Most students don't find it necessary to lock their doors. The **campus is quite safe as long as students use their street smarts** (i.e. walking home from the pub in groups at night, instead of alone)."

Q "First, there's absolutely no crime here. **I've left my door unlocked 24/7** and have never had any problems; the last serious crime the campus experienced was before I enrolled three years ago."

Q "We're in the middle of nowhere and **everyone knows everyone else**. There is a security office, but they are essentially useless and unnecessary. There have been some sexual assaults recently in the town, but none occurred on campus."

Q "The dorms are locked twenty-four hours a day, but the students are so nice they will let anyone in. We have had a few assaults, but mostly internal. **There have been some robberies**, but mostly over breaks."

Q "Three **cheers for Grinnell security officers**! You have very little to fear if you use common sense."

Q "We're in the middle of Iowa. **Security is as good as it gets**."

Q "Health-care on campus is easy to get and the staff is very friendly and helpful. The Health Center covers much of the basics and provides rides to medical offices in town such as the hospital, mental health center, and eye doctor. As for mental health, the **campus provides walk-in counseling and eight free visits to the mental health center** for all students. However, the Health Center has no weekend hours. Also, there is very limited access to a psychiatrist for the town. This is a problem for most Grinnell residents."

Q "I feel pretty safe on campus and will walk by myself at night. Off-campus, I will usually take someone with me. You can also **take advantage of Security's escort system** through which you can call Security at any time of day or night and receive an escort home, no questions asked."

Q "**Security is great here**. I know most of the security guards, at least by sight, and say hi when I see them. They make sure to check up on people who have had too much to drink and make sure they're ok."

Q "Security is lousy. If there were ever a need for safety or a real security team we'd all be slaughtered by the time they got here. There is one really nice, really competent security guard, but the rest of them are confused about their job descriptions. Some think they're cops, others just hold doors open for people. Furthermore, **the director of security is a very confused man**."

Q "I feel very safe on campus; I've left my computer in the library for thirty minutes and returned to find it untouched. **I never even lock the door to my room**. My floor always knows if people come onto the floor that don't belong and will keep an eye out."

Q "**Physical health on campus is pretty good** because a lot of people are into exercise, but mental health on campus is not so awesome. I know a lot of people who aren't doing well emotionally. It might have something to do with all the stress, but I honestly couldn't tell you why."

The College Prowler Take On...
Safety & Security

The security department at Grinnell is pretty small and inactive, but that's mainly because there's not much of a reason for them to exist. Violent crime on campus is unheard of, and Grinnell's Self Governance policy means that security guards are seriously discouraged from poking around in student's lives. Their main job requirements seem to be opening dorm rooms for people who accidentally lock themselves out and clumsily looking up phone numbers for people who call the office. Recently, there have been a few incidents. In the fall of 2002, a few sketchy non-college characters wandered into the dorms and into people's rooms. The campus has since been on twenty-four-hour lockdown, which means that you need your Pioneer-One Card, a college ID, keycard, and debit card for your Grinnell account, in order to gain entrance into any dorm. When security is relaxed, the buildings are open to anyone until 10 p.m. Also in the 2003 school year, there were a few sexual assaults off-campus. The perpetrator, as far as we know, was never apprehended, which worries a lot of students, but there haven't been any incidents for a while. For people who are afraid to walk home at night, the security department provides student volunteers to escort students to their chosen destination.

In the way of health services, one thing that stands out at Grinnell is the large number of students who are diagnosed with depression or other mental health issues on campus. When one prospective student asked a professor what the one thing he would change about Grinnell students would be, the professor responded "I wish they would cheer up." In the spring of 2003, two students committed suicide and an attempted suicide was prevented over the course of two weeks, and another student killed herself at home over Winter Break the same year. The entire community has been on edge ever since. Administration is set on providing more ways for Grinnellians to cope with mental problems, including walk-in counseling sessions, a mental health forum that meets regularly, and eight free sessions with a psychiatrist each year.

The College Prowler™ Grade on

Safety & Security: A-

A high grade in Safety & Security means that students generally feel safe, campus police are visible, blue-light phones and escort services are readily available, and safety precautions are not overly necessary.

Computers

The Lowdown On...
Computers

High-Speed Network?
Yes.

Wireless Network?
Yes.

Number of Labs:
13

Numbers of Computers:
143

Operating Systems:
Windows, Linux, Mac OSX

Free Software (Available on Mathlan):
Mathematica
Maple
Gnu
Java

24-Hour Labs
Norris, Younker, Read, Cleveland, Lazier, Hall B

Charge to Print?
No

Did You Know?]

Many of the Macs in Noyce are being replaced with PCs.

Students Speak Out On...
Computers

> "Most campus-owned buildings are wireless, to some extent. Most students bring their own computer for convenience's sake, but it is not necessary."

Q "Students actively fight to maintain a variety of 24-hour labs. Recent complaints suggest that the **labs might be overcrowded**, but I've never had a problem finding a computer on campus at any hour."

Q "I have my own laptop, and I **definitely recommend bringing a laptop if you bring a computer**. The labs aren't usually that crowded, but they aren't in every dorm. So, having your own computer is a definite plus."

Q "Most **students have their own computers**, so one can almost always find a free computer in the labs, except sometimes during exam week. There is so much work that it would probably be best to have your own computer to work on, but if you don't have a computer you'll be fine."

Q "The network is pretty good here. The only time you will have trouble finding a computer is during finals week, but even then it is still possible to find one. Most students do bring their own computers, easing the strain on the labs and making them most useful for printing and group projects. There is a **decent sized wireless network on campus**, which is steadily increasing in size."

Q "**There is always a computer open**, with the exception being the last two to three weeks of school. Then, there are times when the main labs can fill up, but I never had a problem finding an open computer."

Q "**We have a ton of computer labs**, so if you don't have a computer you can always find one. The only reason I would suggest bringing your own computer is if you want to download music or something, but for papers you can use the labs. They are only crowded around finals."

Q "Although a computer is not necessary, I'd recommend one. Practically **the entire campus has wireless internet coverage**. The network is quite good except when people download viruses. A computer can usually be found in a pinch, but sometimes it's an old one."

Q "While it is convenient to have your own computer, there is **always a computer somewhere on campus** that you can use, although you may have to hunt for one during exam time. The computers are fast, and you can choose between PC, Mac, and Linux boxes."

Q "**If you have a computer, bring it**. However, a lot of people who have their own personal computers still use lab computers to write papers because you can focus better in the labs. I would say the labs are sometimes crowded, but that's just because students don't know where to go. There are a lot of underutilized computers on campus."

Q "**The trend on-campus is to get rid of computer labs**; lots of people don't have computers, but your best bet is to bring one. You'll check your email a lot, and you won't have time to play computer games. I'd recommend having one computer per room."

The College Prowler Take On...
Computers

Despite the fact that Grinnell sometimes seems like a college full of hippies, most of these long-haired barefooted nature freaks happen to be quite computer-savvy. It can get a little frightening when people start referring to you by your username on the college network, but Grinnell provides some very useful services when it comes to technology. Every Grinnell student has to attend a technology session during Student Orientation week. In Orientation, Internet Technology Service student employees give you your username, which generally consists of the first seven or eight letters of your name, tell you how to hook up your computer to the Ethernet, and then show you how to get into your email account. This is only the beginning. Upon poking around the web page, you'll find a Directory, informally referred to as Stalker Net that will not only allow you to look up the address and phone number of any Grinnell student or faculty member, but also give you their major, username, class year, home address, and ID photo. Fortunately, most of this information is only available through computers that are plugged into the campus network. On Grinnell's faculty page, you can find links to web pages that many of the professors have set up for each course. You can even check your grades online through Pioneer Web.

"The powers that be" at Grinnell adhere to the overall campus dependence on technology and go to great lengths to accommodate the students. Many of the dorms have computer labs on the first floor that are always unlocked. While these fill up pretty quickly around finals time, open computers can usually be found in the computer labs in academic buildings, and there are also computers available in many of the science lab rooms. Both Macs and PCs are common, but can't always be found in the same computer lab for some reason. Computer viruses run rampant on campus, but Internet and Technology Service employees are usually able to fix them, even if you have to haul your computer tower down the street for them to work on it.

The College Prowler™ Grade on Computers: B+

A high grade in Computers designates that computer labs are available, the computer network is easily accessible, and the campus' computing technology is up-to-date.

Facilities

The Lowdown On...
Facilities

Student Center:
The Forum

Athletic Center:
The Physical Education Complex (PEC). Also, a new gymnasium is being built.

Libraries:
Yes, there are two.

Popular Places to Chill:
The Forum
Bob's Underground Cafe

Campus Size in Acres:
120 acres

What Is There to Do On Campus?
When you need to take a break from studying, there are pool tables in the Harris Center and the Forum, a climbing wall and swimming pool in the PEC, art shows at Faulkner gallery in Bucksbaum, and frequent concerts including Classical, student, and professional performances. Punk bands from across the nation are booked regularly.

Movie Theatre on Campus?
Yes, there's Harris Cinema in the Harris Center. Movies are also shown in the Forum every weekend and special interest films are usually played in ARH.

Bar on Campus?
No

Bowling on Campus?
No

Coffeehouse on Campus?
Bob's Underground Cafe, in the basement of Main

Favorite Things to Do:
Many students take advantage of the free movies in Harris and on the South Lounge of the Forum on weekends. Plays (also free) are put on both by the college theatre department and the Grinnell Independent Theatre group, but tickets (which can usually be found at the box office in Bucksbaum) tend to go rather quickly. The numerous bands that Grinnell brings to the stage also tend to attract a large crowd.

Students Speak Out On...
Facilities

> "Everything at Grinnell is top-notch. I might complain about the computer labs if anything, but there's almost always a computer open somewhere."

- "**The PEC is awesome**. It is very retro, but they are about to tear it down because the administration workers here are a forward thinking bunch and are much more concerned with the potential student of ten years from now than they are with the current student. Students hang out in the forum, I guess. Yeah, I guess all the facilities suck on campus except the science building, the theater building (which is awesome) and the showers in the PEC."

- "The campus is very well-funded and **Grinnell is in the midst of building a new athletic facility and student center**. I've always found the facilities adequate to serve about any purpose I could want."

- "**The facilities at Grinnell are above par.** The athletic center is above par, except the equipment in the weight room is a little outdated."

- "Currently, **the campus is in the middle of major renovations**, so very soon there will be a new student center and a new Physical Education Complex."

- "The Forum Grill is really satisfying and has lots of good stuff to eat. **The computer labs are nice**, especially the ones in the academic buildings."

Q "I think the facilities are nice. Still, the College is making an effort to improve them. I was pleased with the old dorms; still, the College built new dorms. I was pleased with the Forum (student center); now, the College is building a new Campus Center. I was pleased with the PEC (athletic building); however, the college felt that building a new one was necessary. **Grinnell seems very concerned with keeping up-to-date, for better or for worse**. "

Q "**The soccer fields are the best I've ever seen**. The new athletic center should be very nice, but the current one is good too. The computer labs on campus are good too, but they get a bit crowded during hell and finals weeks."

Q "**The facilities are forever a work in progress**. There are new athletic and student centers being built, not that students are too happy about that."

Q "We have nice buildings here. **Our new science and art buildings are very pleasing** to the eye. Also, they fit very well with the atmosphere on campus."

The College Prowler Take On...
Facilities

Currently, Grinnell is going through a massive revamping of its current facilities. Within the next few years (by 2007 or so) many buildings that are now near and dear to Grinnellians' hearts will either disappear or be altered beyond recognition. The first step in the on campus rebuilding campaign was the construction of East Campus. The process continued this summer with the demolition of Darby, a gymnasium that was built in 1942, and was a central and highly recognizable part of the Grinnell landscape. After the current Physical Education Center, which contains numerous amenities, including a pool, climbing wall, weight room, and track, is torn down, some of the bricks from the current Darby and the iconic torch on the side of the building will be transplanted to a new "Darby" gym in the new PEC. Although intentions were good, the move failed to appease the student body, and many students voiced their opinions by sporting "Save Darby" T-shirts.

The next major project will be the construction of a sprawling, modern Campus Center. The current Health Center and Stonewall Resource Center even had to be torn down to make room for this behemoth. After its construction, both cafeterias, most of the multicultural club offices, an art gallery and KDIC, and the Grinnell radio station will be moved into this building. The new buildings will be built in a completely different style from that of Grinnell's older Gothic architecture, rather than the red and black brick stonework that decorates most of North and South campus (there are few things that can make a lecture building look cooler than gargoyles over the doors) a newer more modern apparatus will line the walls of our campus facilities and eateries. I suppose that, even in Iowa, college campuses inevitably change with the times.

The College Prowler™ Grade on
Facilities: B

A high Facilities grade indicates that the campus is aesthetically pleasing and well-maintained; facilities are state-of-the-art, and libraries are exceptional. Other determining factors include the quality of both athletic and student centers and an abundance of things to do on campus.

Campus Dining

The Lowdown On...
Campus Dining

Freshman Meal Plan Requirement?
Yes

Meal Plan Average Cost:
$1,833 per semester

Places to Grab a Bite with Your Meal Plan

Quad Dining Hall
Location: Main Hall
Food: Basic Cafeteria Food
Favorite Dish: Chicken Patty Parmesan
Hours: Weekdays 7:15-9:00 a.m., 11:15-12:45 p.m., 4:45 p.m. - 6:30 p.m. Saturday: 11:45 a.m. – 1:00 p.m., 5:30 p.m. - 6:30 p.m. Sunday 11:45 a.m. – 1:00 p.m., 5:30 p.m. - 6:45 p.m.

Cowles Dining Hall
Location: Cowles Hall
Food: Cafeteria
Favorite Dish: Hot Wings
Hours: Weekdays 7:15 a.m. - 9:00 a.m., 11:15 a.m. - 12:45 p.m., 5:30 p.m. - 7:15 p.m. Saturday 9:00 a.m. - 10:00 a.m., 11:45 p.m.-1:00 p.m., 5:30 p.m. - 6:30 p.m.

Sunday 9:00 a.m. - 10:00 a.m., 11:45 p.m. - 12:45 p.m., 5:30 p.m. - 6:45 p.m.

The Forum Grill
(Accepts Dining Dollars)
Location: Central Campus
Food: Pizza and Deli Fare
Favorite Dish: Cheese Pizza
Hours: Sunday 1:00 p.m. - 12:00 midnight
Monday - Thursday 7:45 a.m. - 12:00 midnight
Friday 7:45 a.m. - 1:00 a.m.
Saturday 10:00 a.m. - 1:00 a.m.

Grab and Go
Location: Cowles Hall
Food: Sack Lunches
Favorite Dish: Hummus
Hours: Monday-Thursday 10:00 a.m. - 4:30 p.m.
Friday 10:00 a.m. - 2:00 p.m.

Student Favorites:
The Forum

24-Hour On-Campus Eating?
No.

Other Options:
Every dorm has at least one kitchen that students can use at their convenience. Keeping a stash of frozen pizzas is always a good idea, unless you live in Norris. The Norris oven has been known to set off the fire alarm anytime someone tries to cook a pizza. So, if you end up in Norris, go to Dibble to for any baking endeavors.

Did You Know?

In the Fall of 2004, manyfirst-years chose the Super 21 Meal Plan, which includes 21 meals per week, at either cafeteria, and $125 Dining Dollars that can be used at the Forum Grill.

Students Speak Out On...
Campus Dining

> "The food in the dining hall is terrible. It would be much better if dining services would spend as much time on the food as they do thinking of more diabolical ways to cheat students out of money!"

Q "Food on campus is on a one-month-main-menu rotation, there's always a salad and sandwich line. So, with some creativity, **the food's not too bad**."

Q "**The food is awful**, but the quad cafeteria looks exactly like Hogwarts dining hall, so the ambiance makes up for it."

Q "The food at Grinnell is pretty good. I have had better dorm food and I have had worse. **Dining service employees are very open to feedback**. Moreover, there is always a vegetarian option, a vegan option, salad bar, sandwich bar, soup, cereal, bagels, and ice cream."

Q "The dining halls aren't as bad as everyone makes them out to be. **There isn't much variety**, but the food isn't terrible. There is also a Pizza Hut in town that is really close to campus (close enough to walk) that is really fun to go to."

Q "The dining halls are okay sometimes. Also, the **forum is good for late night cravings.**"

Q "**The two dining halls are decent**, but not wonderful. The college seems to spend its money more on equipment and staff than on dining services. With that being said, there is a new dining hall being constructed that should be completed in a year or two. It will mean that the college will have a centralized dining hall instead of two separate, isolated ones, which will be good because I will be able to see my friends on the other end of campus at meals. It will also mean new equipment for dining services, which should equate to better food."

Q "Food on campus is bad—**it's just plain bad!** They try really hard, and the cooks are really nice. Basically, it's a bunch of Midwestern women trying to make something that the European chef likes. They are constantly trying to mass produce meals that cannot be successfully expanded to feed that many people. The only way to get good food is to walk a few blocks to Fareway, come back to your dorm, and cook for yourself."

Q "If you have to be in the dining hall you could assemble something edible from the options they do provide for you. Also, if you like salad you might be okay. Sometimes the lettuce is crusty, but **they try hard to keep fresh vegetables around**. There are no restaurants on campus, although there is a coffee shop open at night with fresh bagels and cream cheese. The coffee shop is one of the few places on campus that I feel drips with personality and flows with character."

Q "Uh, the dining hall food is anything but tasty. **The food never tastes bad**, but it is seldom tastes good. If anything, you'll end up getting creative with your diet, concocting your own pasta sauce from salad bar tomatoes and the spice rack, or making a quesadilla from the deli bar and a microwave, the list goes on. There are several types of coffee on campus, but Bob's Underground Café serves the best. Also, be sure to try the 'leslie' or the 'bastard' at Bob's, both are stellar variations of the traditional bagel."

Q "On-campus food is terrible. However, the alternatives are acceptable. It's a ten-minute walk into town, and there is also the **wonderful Forum Grill in the middle of campus**."

Q "Food at the **dining halls is a tad bland** and really overpriced, but most students that don't mind mediocre food stay on the dining plan.

The College Prowler Take On...
Campus Dining

In general, most of the student body would agree that the current dining situation at Grinnell is quite dismal, but students make the most of it. There are a lot of options and, as far as I know, no Grinnell students have starved to death or gone on a hunger strike because of contaminated stuffed bell peppers. The two college dining halls at this point ('04) are Cowles on North Campus and Quad on South. In terms of the food they serve, the two are almost identical. Both eateries have a main line, which includes various main courses and hot side dishes each day. The main lines include such delicacies as chicken patty Parmesan, manicotti, pasta with alfredo sauce, "jojo fries", and vegetables and rice. Also, each offers a salad bar, a sandwich bar, cereal table, desserts, bagels, bread, tortillas, fruits, and more for picky students who find the day's options in the mainline unsatisfactory. The sundae bar gives sweet-toothed diners infinite options for creative and delicious desserts. Also, there are always dishes on the main line for vegans and vegetarians, spinach casserole and veggie submarines to name a few.

Some people have intense loyalties to one dining hall or the other and, in terms of atmosphere, the two are very different. Cowles is located on the first floor of a residence hall, and is designed much like a traditional college cafeteria. Also, the close setup of the salad bar and main line are much more conducive to getting food quickly. For some though, Quad holds a more bohemian appeal. The building the dining hall is located in was actually meant to be a church. The high vaulted, arched ceiling and stained glass windows are usually a dead giveaway for visiting parents and friends. Also opposed to the efficient uniformity of Cowles is the furniture in the Quad, which includes a hodgepodge of tables that might as well have been taken straight out of a Harry Potter movie. However, the differences will soon be a moot point because the college is planning to do away with Cowles and Quad to make way for a single enormous dining hall in the new Campus Center. For now, other options for food on campus include The Forum Grill, Bob's Underground, and Grab and Go. All these delectable eateries provide Grinnell students a scrumptious getaway from the monotony that is Grinnell dining.

The College Prowler™ Grade on Campus Dining: D+

Our grade on Campus Dining addresses the quality of both school-owned dining halls and independent on-campus restaurants as well as the price, availability, and variety of food.

Off-Campus Dining

The Lowdown On...
Off-Campus Dining

Restaurant Prowler: Popular Places to Eat!

AJ's Steakhouse
Food: American
Address: Hwy 146 north of I-80
Phone: (641) 236-0386
Price: $20 and under per person

Back Alley Deli
Food: Sandwiches
Address: 917 Broad St.
Phone: (641) 236-3010
Price: $5 and under per person

Cafe Phoenix
Food: Upscale restaurant
Address: 834 Park St.
Phone: (641) 236-3657
Price: $30 and under per person

China Sea
Food: Chinese
Address: 714 Fourth Ave.
Phone: (641) 236-8831
Price: $10 and under per person

Chuong Garden
Food: Chinese
Address: 915 Broad St.
Phone: (641) 236-9900
Price: $10 and under per

person
Price: Under $10
Hours: Monday through Thursday: 7 a.m.-12 a.m., Friday 7 a.m.-1 a.m., Saturday 8 a.m.-1 a.m., Sunday 8 a.m.-12 a.m.

Danish Maid Bakery
Food: Pastries
Address: 818 Fourth Ave.
Phone: (641) 236-4145
Price: $5 and under per person

Dari Barn
Food: Ice Cream and American
Address: 1810 Sixth Ave.
Phone: (641) 236-7828
Price: $5 and under per person

Depot Crossing
Food: American
Address: 1014 Third Ave.
Phone: 236-6886
Price: $15 and under per person

Godfather's Pizza
Food: Pizza
Address: 800 4th Ave Grinnell
Phone: (641) 236-6516
Price: $10 and under per person

Grinnell Coffee Company
Food: Coffee and Appetizers
Address: 915 Main St.
Phone: (641) 236-0710
Price: $5 and under per person

Kelcy's Fine Foods
Food: American
Address: 812 Sixth Ave.
Phone: (641) 236-3132
Price: $15 and under per person

The Main Squeeze
Food: Smoothies and Wraps
Address: 829 Broad St.
Phone (641) 236-7474
Price: $10 and under per person

Michael's
Food: Italian
Address: 720 Fifth Ave.
Phone: (641) 236-4211
Price: $20 and under per person

Pagliai's Pizza
Food: Pizza
Address: 816 Fifth Avenue
Phone: (641) 236-5331
Price: $10 and under per person

Pizza Hut
Food: Pizza
Address: 1033 Broad St.
Phone: (641) 236-7737
Price: $10 and under

Saint's Rest Coffeehouse
Food: Coffee and Pastries
Address: 919 Broad St.
Phone: (641) 236-6014
Price: $5 and under per person

Satchmo's
Food: Pizza and Nachos
Deliveries only
Phone: (641) 236-0183
Price: $6.99 - $15.99 per pizza, plus delivery charge ($1)

Subway
Food: Sandwiches
Address: 1102 West Grinnell
Phone: (641) 236-7884
Price: $5 and under per pers

Taco John's
Food: Mexican
Address: 1020 West St. Grinnell
Phone: (641) 236-4863
Price: $5 and under per person

Westside Diner
Food: American
Address: 226 West Sixth Ave.
Phone: (641) 236-9117
Price: $15 and under per person

Student Favorites:
Saint's Rest Coffeehouse
Pagliai's Pizza
Dari Barn
Danish Maid Bakery
The Main Squeeze

Closest Grocery Stores:

McNally's Foods
1021 Main St.
(641) 236-3166

Fareway
1020 Spring St.
(641) 236-4868

Hy-Vee Food and Pharmacy
320 West St.
(641) 236-6584

Juli's Health and More Food Store
931 West St.
(641) 236-7376

Did You Know?

Best Pizza:
Pagliai's Pizza

Best Chinese:
Chuong Garden

Best Breakfast:
Westside Diner

Best Wings:
AJ's Steakhouse

Best Healthy:
The Main Squeeze

Best Place to Take Your Parents:
The Phoenix Cafe

Late-Night Dining:

The Danish Maid finishes baking it's pastries at 2 a.m., which has led to a tradition aptly named "The 2:00 AM Bakery Run." This is a good thing to remember when you're up late at night writing a paper, but the bakery opens late on Saturday and Sunday, so you'll have to go on a weeknight.

Satchmo's pizza delivers straight to your room between 9:00 p.m. and 1:00 a.m.

Students Speak Out On...
Off-Campus Dining

"The food in town isn't great, but there's lots of variety if you like pizza and hamburgers. What genuine American doesn't?"

Q "**There are a variety of cheap restaurants in the area** (Subway, Pizza Hut) and two or three nice joints for special occasions (The Phoenix, Depot, and Pagliai's come to mind)."

Q "There are not very many different places on campus to eat, but when you get sick of eating on campus, off-campus dining is a nice opportunity to support local commerce. **One of the most popular places is Pag's,** which is a local pizza joint with pretty decent pizza at a more-than-decent price. There are also a few nicer restaurants off-campus, depending on what you are looking for. A.J.'s steakhouse, the Depot (a restaurant situated in the old train station in town), Kelcy's, and Cafe Phoenix are definitely all worth trying."

Q "**The Depot, Chuong Garden, Pag's, and Café Phoenix are all student favorites**. There are also two coffee shops in town that students frequent. The restaurants are quite good, and are a nice break from the dining halls."

Q "**AJ's is a very good place if you like steak** (you get to grill your own) and good Thai food is about a half hour away (Thai Basil)."

Q "The good spots are Café Phoenix and the depot. **A&M is great for breakfast**!"

Q "There are a number of pizza places around. Some are okay, but no restaurants in town (on a college budget) are that great. Maybe Chuoong Gardens would be ok, but I wouldn't push it. **Cook for yourself, its cheaper and more enjoyable**. "

Q "**Westside Diner is a good restaurant**. It's the town' most underrated eatery in my opinion."

Q "Off-campus dining is excellent. **Pagliai's pizzeria is good for pizza**, and there is a new Chinese restaurant that is amazing. For the more main streamed tastes, there is a McDonald's and a Subway. Dari Barn, a ten-minute walk from campus, is a private fast-food place that has good food and better ice cream."

The College Prowler Take On...
Off-Campus Dining

While off-campus dining in and around Grinnell is lacking a bit in diversity, it's certainly a viable alternative to campus dining. It's easy to find a good pizza in town, and whoever thought up Satchmo's 9 p.m. to 1 a.m. deserves to win a Nobel Prize. People looking for a good solid Midwestern meal will surely not be disappointed. With this being said, off-campus dining is more of a social event than a culinary adventure. While the pizza at Pagliai's is awesome, the best part about going there is forgetting about upcoming deadlines and academic hassles. It is not uncommon for five or so Grinnell students to take a stroll down to 'Pag's' and forget, if at least for an hour, that they all have term papers due in the morning.

Furthermore, some restaurants that have been around for a while have become unofficially linked to the college. Saint's Rest is owned by a former Grinnell student, and Grinnellians constantly use it as a study haven. You would be hard-pressed to find a customer there around finals week that doesn't have a text book in front of them. Pagliai's serves mostly townies and seems to primarily employ high school students. It does, however, serve as a hub for Grinnell college student gatherings. Occasionally, professors treat their students to a meal there at the end of each semester. The Phoenix Cafe is also well-known on campus, but it is notorious for the ridiculously expensive menu and it's the most common restaurant that Grinnell students take their parents to. Last, but certainly not least, is the Dari Barn. It's safe to say that 9:00 p.m. Dari Barn ice cream runs have become a Grinnell pastime, even if they could never get the name right.

The College Prowler™ Grade on
Off-Campus Dining: B-

A high off-campus dining grade implies that off-campus restaurants are affordable, accessible, and worth visiting. Other factors include the variety of cuisine and the availability of alternative options (vegetarian, vegan, Kosher, etc.).

Campus Housing

The Lowdown On...
Campus Housing

Room Types:

Room types include Closet Singles, Singles, Doubles, Triples and Quads.

Closet Singles are tiny singles with just about enough room for a bed, desk, dresser, and chair. Juniors and sophomores tend to live in singles. Closet singles are not assigned to first years.

Larger singles, or regular singles, are sometimes actual doubles that only have one person assigned to them. These have plenty of room, but are harder to get than closet singles or traditional doubles. Under normal circumstances, first years don't live in regular singles.

Doubles have enough room and furniture for two students, and are about the same size or larger than an average bedroom. Most first-years end up in these.

Triples are comparable in size to a living room, rather than bedroom; some are split into three rooms, including two or three small bedrooms and a common room. Sometimes, a few lucky first years are assigned triples.

Quads are designed for four people and usually have more than one room. The most common design consists of two tiny bedrooms, basically with room for a bunk bed and a dresser each, and a small common room.

Students in Singles:
50%

Students in Doubles:
45%

Students in Triples / Suites:
5%

Dormitories

Main
Floors: 3
Total Occupancy: 51
Bathrooms:
Lounges: 3
Kitchens: 1
Laundry Room: Yes
Air Conditioning: No
Co-Ed: By alternating rooms
Percentage of First-Year Students: 31%
Room Types: Singles and Doubles
Special Features: Main has an elevator and is in the same building as Bob's Underground, Gardiner Lounge and Quad dining hall.

Cleveland
Floors: 4
Total Occupancy: 53
Bathrooms:
Lounges: 4
Kitchens: 1
Laundry Room: No
Computer Lab: Yes
Air Conditioning: No
Co-Ed: By alternating rooms
Percentage of First-Year Students: 32%
Room Types: Singles, Doubles
Special Features: Big-screen TV in two of the lounges

James
Floors: 5
Total Occupancy: 58
Bathrooms:
Lounges: 4
Kitchens: 1
Laundry Room: No
Computer Lab: No
Air Conditioning: No
Co-Ed: By alternating rooms - 3rd floor is all male
Percentage of First-Year Students: 38%
Room Types: Singles, Doubles
Special Features: Non-Smoking

Haines
Floors: 4
Total Occupancy: 66
Bathrooms:

Lounges: 3
Kitchens: 1
Laundry Room: No
Computer Lab: No
Air Conditioning: No
Co-Ed: By alternating rooms - 3rd floor is all female
Percentage of First-Year Students: 20%
Room Types: Singles, Doubles, Triples and Quads
Special Features: Pit is floor drawand Sulzberger, Wellness Floor, sinks in some rooms, inoperable fireplaces in some rooms, internet access, first year students live on specific floors

Loose
Floors: 4
Total Occupancy: 96
Bathrooms:
Lounges: 3
Kitchens: 5
Laundry Room: Yes
Computer Lab: Yes
Air Conditioning: No
Co-Ed: By alternating rooms
Percentage of First-Year Students: 25%
Room Types: Singles and Doubles
Special Features: Piano in lounge

Younker
Floors: 4
Total Occupancy: 113
Bathrooms:
Lounges: 4
Kitchens: 2
Laundry Room: Yes
Computer Lab: Yes
Air Conditioning: No
Co-Ed: By alternating rooms – Pit is single sex female
Percentage of First-Year Students: 33%
Room Types: Singles and Doubles
Special Features: Piano in Lounge

Smith
Floors: 4
Total Occupancy: 52
Bathrooms:
Lounges: 3
Kitchens: 1
Laundry Room: No
Computer Lab: No
Air Conditioning: No
Co-Ed: By alternating rooms – annex is single sex female
Percentage of First-Year Students: 38%
Room Types: Singles, Doubles and Triples
Special Features: Substance Free, Pit is Group Draw

Langan
Floors: 4
Total Occupancy: 52
Bathrooms:
Lounges: 4
Kitchens: 1
Laundry Room: No
Computer Lab: No
Air Conditioning: Yes
Co-Ed: By alternating rooms
Percentage of First-Year Students: 50%

Room Types: Singles, Doubles and Triples

Special Features: Non-Smoking

Rawson
Floors: 4
Total Occupancy: 32
Bathrooms:
Lounges: 4
Kitchens: 1
Laundry Room: No
Computer Lab: No
Air Conditioning: No
Co-Ed: By alternating floors: Pit and 2nd are male, 3rd is female
Percentage of First-Year Students: 47%
Room Types: Singles, Doubles and Triples
Special Features: Non-Smoking, Piano in lounge

Gates
Floors: 5
Total Occupancy: 36
Bathrooms:
Lounges: 4
Kitchens: 1
Laundry Room: No
Computer Lab: No
Air Conditioning: No
Co-Ed: Alternating single sex and coed floors: pit is female, 1st is co-ed, 2nd is all male, 3rd is all female
Percentage of First-Year Students: 44%
Room Types: Singles, Doubles and Triples
Special Features: 4th and 5th floors are Group Draw. Gates tower is considered an icon of Grinnell, and appears in Grinnell pamphlets everywhere.

Clark
Floors: 4
Total Occupancy: 52
Bathrooms:
Lounges: 4
Kitchens: 1
Laundry Room: No
Computer Lab: No
Air Conditioning: No
Co-Ed: by alternating rooms
Percentage of First-Year Students: 27%
Room Types: Singles, Doubles and Triples
Special Features: In close proximity to classes

Dibble
Floors: 4
Total Occupancy: 40
Bathrooms:
Lounges: 3
Kitchens: 1
Laundry Room: Yes
Computer Lab: No
Air Conditioning: No
Co-Ed: by alternating rooms and single sex floor – annex is male
Percentage of First-Year Students: 38%
Room Types: Singles, Doubles and Triples
Special Features: Consistently known as an active social dorm

Cowles
Floors: 2
Total Occupancy: 45
Bathrooms:
Lounges: 2
Kitchens: 1
Laundry Room: No
Computer Lab: No
Air Conditioning: No
Co-Ed: by alternating rooms
Percentage of First-Year Students: 33%
Room Types: Singles, Doubles and Quads
Special Features: Right above Cowles dining hall

Norris
Floors: 4
Total Occupancy: 97
Bathrooms:
Lounges: 4
Kitchens: 1
Laundry Room: No
Computer Lab: Yes
Air Conditioning: Yes
Co-Ed: by alternating rooms
Percentage of Men/Women: 64%
Room Types: Singles and Doubles
Special Features: 1st floor is Group Draw, Piano in Lounge

Lazier
Floors: 5
Total Occupancy: 50
Bathrooms:
Lounges: 6
Kitchens: 4
Laundry Room: Yes
Computer Lab: No
Air Conditioning: Yes
Co-Ed: by alternating rooms
Percentage of First-Year Students: 28%
Room Types: Singles and Doubles
Special Features: Elevator, Piano in Lounge, Non-Smoking, Unorthodox Name

Hall B
Floors: 3
Total Occupancy: 69
Bathrooms:
Lounges: 3
Kitchens: 1
Laundry Room: Yes
Computer Lab: Yes
Air Conditioning: Yes
Co-Ed: by alternating rooms
Percentage of First-Year Students: 16%
Room Types: Singles and Doubles
Special Features: Elevator, Non-Smoking

Rose
Floors: 3
Total Occupancy: 69
Bathrooms:
Lounges: 3
Kitchens: 1
Laundry Room: Yes
Computer Lab: No
Air Conditioning: Yes
Co-Ed: North and South 2nd floors are female, South 1st and 3rd and North 2nd floors are male
Percentage of First-Year Students: 30%

Room Types: Singles and Doubles

Special Features: North First is Floor Draw, Non-Smoking, Elevator

East
Floors: 3
Total Occupancy: 71
Bathrooms:
Lounges: 3
Kitchens: 1
Laundry Room: Yes
Computer Lab: No
Air Conditioning: Yes
Co-Ed: by alternating rooms
Percentage of First-Year Students: 11%
Room Types: Doubles and Singles

Special Features: Non-Smoking, Elevator

Number of Dormitories:
19

Undergrads on Campus:
1,314 (93%)

University-Owned Apartments:
0

Bed Type
Extra long twin

Available for Rent
Mini-fridges, Lofts

Cleaning Service?
In public areas and bathrooms

What You Get
Each student receives a bed, desk, chair, bookshelf, Ethernet jack, curtains, dresser, phone, free campus and local phone calls

Also Available:
Non-Smoking Housing, Substance-Free Housing, Special-Interest Housing

Did You Know?

North and South campuses are connected by a series of underground maintenance tunnels that student's aren't permitted to use.

In doubles, it's usually possible to bunk (stack) the beds.

Students Speak Out On...
Campus Housing

> "East campus dorms are still new and hold a stigma, but they are air-conditioned unlike most of the others."

Q "**The dorms are extravagant**, with the exception of Norris, a temporary building that's just a horrible sight. The floors are small and the students living together have very tight-knit relationships. Don't expect to get a room to yourself before your third year, though."

Q "**The dorms are quite good**. There really are no dorms to avoid."

Q "All the dorms are pretty nice; **you really can't go wrong with any of them**. There is the very occasional tiny 'shoe box' room, but generally there is plenty of space and they are pretty comfortable."

Q "**Norris is the worst dorm**, and the rest of the dorms are all about personal taste. I like Main the best and I always will. Main's a party dorm full of lots of hard core party kids and drug users. There are few, if any jocks, so things don't get brutalized too often. Also at Main, you have the dining hall and a formal lounge on the first floor and in the basement we have Gardener (The scene for indie rock shows), bob's coffee shop, and the laundry room. It's easy to get through an Iowa winter in Main. Just don't leave the building unless you have a class."

Q "Norris has a bad reputation as being the worst dorm, and it isn't terribly nice, but it makes up for that in the atmosphere. I think **Norris is the most social dorm on campus**. The new east campus residence halls feel very sterile."

Q "The dorms are very nice, the rooms are spacious, and the lounges are great too. **There aren't any dorms to avoid**, and there isn't a specific senior dorm or a freshman dorm. All classes get mixed together, which is great for the first-years because they can talk to juniors and seniors about which classes to take, which professors are the best, and possibly even get old course books for cheap."

Q "Norris is an older dorm with lots of character, which makes it my favorite, but many people prefer the newer dorms in East campus because they have bigger rooms. East dorms feel too hygienic for me, though. North and **South Campuses have great rooms, but you have to know the character of the dorms**. Norris is full of cracked-out first-years, Cowles has lots of 'Dungeon and Dragons' type of people; Dibble, Clark, and Younker all have lots of Jocks, and Smith students are conservative about everything. South Campus, Loose students have, well, loose attitudes about everything, Cleveland is constantly smoky from the lounge, which always has a couple people smoking pot in it. Finally, Main is more slanted toward the drug users and intellectuals."

Q "The dorms, altogether, are quite nice. North and South campuses date back to the early 1900's and have quite a bit of character, whereas **East Campus is brand-new**, which provides its own set of advantages. The only dorms I would suggest staying away from are Cleveland and Norris, mostly because of the great amount of smoke within each."

Q "**The dorms here are very clean and not at all crowded**. I would personally suggest avoiding South campus if you do not like smoke. Also, East campus is new so it is always a fine choice to live there."

The College Prowler Take On...
Campus Housing

Grinnell uses a room draw system for selecting dorm rooms, in which your chances of getting the room you want are based on an ingenious mix of seniority and luck. Every spring, each student in the college is randomly assigned a number from one to however many students there happen to be that year. Then, on one Saturday near the end of the year, each class lines up in turn outside of the concert hall in Harris to pick rooms. The juniors with the lowest numbers pick first, then the highest juniors, then the lowest sophomores, etc, all the way down to the highest numbers of the freshman class. If you have selected a roommate or two, the lowest number is used and you go into the concert hall together to pick out a room. Floor plans for all of the dorms are taped to tables labeled with the name of each building, and you simply sign on the line for the room number you want and hand over your sticker to the faculty member behind the table then, voila! You have a room. If only finding an apartment in the real world was this easy.

Since incoming freshmen are obviously not around to pick a room or specific dorm, the college selects their rooms for them. Never fear; many rooms are reserved before room draw, so they aren't left with the leftover scraps of upper classmen. While some first-years end up randomly scattered across campus, a good majority of them end up in Norris. To be frank, Norris closely resembles a Nazi prison camp and is located at the very northern tip of campus, where students have to take a commercial jet in order to get to all of the academic buildings, not to mention Burling, and The Forum. Norris is, in all actuality, a great place for first years to end up. There is nothing that can cement friendships faster than shoving sixty or so nervous and bewildered eighteen-year-olds into the same building. Also, in August and September, you will learn to appreciate that you are in one of the few dorms on campus that has air conditioning—see, there's bound to be some redeeming quality wherever you may end up your first year.

The College Prowler™ Grade on
Campus Housing: A-

A high Campus Housing grade indicates that dorms are clean, well-maintained, and spacious. Other determining factors include variety of dorms, proximity to classes, and social atmosphere.

Off-Campus Housing

The Lowdown On...
Off-Campus Housing

Undergrads in Off-Campus Housing:
210

Average Rent for a 1BR:
$200/month

Average Rent for a 2BR:
$400/month

Best Time to Look for a Place
Spring or Fall

Popular Areas:
Downtown
Within two blocks West of campus
Park St.

Where to Look:
The Campus Memo
The bulletin board in the post office

Students Speak Out On...
Off-Campus Housing

"You have to be off-campus to be off of the meal plan. It's a lot cheaper to live off campus. It's really hard though. Don't think about living off-campus until you're a senior."

Q "**Off-campus housing is convenient and affordable** as one could hope for, but Grinnell requires you to live in dorms (with some exceptions) until your senior year. I thought this would be horrendous but, in all actuality, it makes for more diverse social groups (i.e. your floor during freshman year will not be in a freshmen dorm where everyone's drunk, noisy, and rude 24/7). Freshmen are all full members of the community."

Q "You can live off-campus in a language house or a theme house sponsored by the college. **Most students, however, live on campus all four years**. Some seniors live in apartments downtown, which is really convenient if you want to have a party or a taste of the 'real world' living before you graduate."

Q "You simply can't do it. At least **not until you are a senior**. The college puts a lot of effort into keeping the campus residential, and I really like that about Grinnell. Everyone is on campus, and there's really no reason to leave."

Q "If you get a fun group of people together it could be worth it to live off-campus, but **most students prefer to live on campus** until their junior or senior year."

Q "**Off-campus housing is not available until junior or senior year.** Most students live on campus and most are happy with that."

Q "The school used to have lots of off-campus housing, but is slowly but surely getting rid of it all. Granted, the dorms are pretty nice, but **most people are willing to live off-campus to save money** and to avoid the dining halls."

Q "**There is almost no off-campus housing**, although students wish there were."

The College Prowler Take On...
Off-Campus Housing

Grinnell administration prides itself on making our college a residential one, so they try to discourage students from living off-campus as much as possible. Students aren't even permitted to live off-campus until their junior year, and in the past few years off-campus college-owned houses have been removed in order to make room for other facilities. Students who choose to live off-campus must have written permission from the Student Affairs office. Most students choose to remain in the dorms for all four years and, when they move out, very few students choose to live alone. However, if you do choose to live off-campus, it's not horrifically expensive. There are a few landlords who own houses that have been converted into apartments. While these houses are often a bit run down, they do offer extra possibilities for partying and, with a few roommates, most students end up paying $200-$300 per month. Most importantly, the houses are generally within a few blocks of campus.

Unfortunately, the options for renting apartments near Grinnell are fairly limited. The only apartment building in Grinnell is the Brande, which is about two blocks south of campus. The rooms in Brande are generous in size and cost about $400 per month. More apartments are located over the Pub, and these are quite convenient for parties because the neighbors downstairs in the bar obviously won't complain. As for the off-campus college-owned houses that remain, most of them are language houses, including Spanish, French, Russian and Chinese. Only two other houses are allotted in groups each year, and they have to apply to get the house and convince administration that they will somehow offer a service to the Grinnell community. For now, we have the International Gourmet House and Dag House. Gourmet House recently won the building over the residents of Musik Haus. There's always a chance that the musicians might win the place back from the Gourmets, who have promised to publish a free recipe book by the end of the year and cook food for the occasional food bazaars hosted by the International Student Organization. Dag House is controlled by a student group focused on the sport of fighting with foam swords, and has taken up an annual project of hosting a small Renaissance Fair.

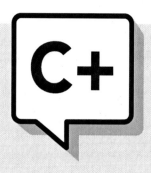

The College Prowler™ Grade on
Off-Campus Housing: C+

A high grade in Off-Campus Housing indicates that apartments are of high quality, close to campus, affordable, and easy to secure.

Diversity

The Lowdown On...
Diversity

American Indian:
5%

Asian or Pacific Islander:
4%

African American:
3%

Hispanic:
3%

White:
66%

International:
10%

Unknown:
12%

Out of State:
86%

Political Activity

Many students believe that there is too little political diversity on campus. Most students are moderate to radical left-wing, and republicans and right-wingers often feel that their views are cast aside too swiftly by their peers. However, when it comes to the views on the Left, you will find anything from devout democrats to outright anarchists, and every person in between.

Gay Tolerance

Grinnell is amazing when it comes to gay tolerance, and is one of the most open colleges in the country. Many gay, lesbian, and bisexual students at Grinnell come out of the closet to their peers before they can come out to their parents. Organizations like Stonewall Coalition serve as hubs for the homosexual community, and students harassing others on the basis of their sexual preference is unheard of and would not be tolerated. However, there have been frequent complaints of people who live in town, particularly high school students, harassing random Grinnell students in passing with derogatory references to homosexuality.

Most Popular Religions

The Christian community on campus tends to be the most visible through student groups, but other religions are widely accepted. There also seems to be a sizable Atheist and Agnostic community, and while these groups don't tend to make much noise, some religious students are occasionally scrutinized by others who have anti-religious views.

Economic Status

While there are a good number of upper-class and upper-middle-class students at Grinnell, due to the college's need-blind admissions policy, many people from underprivileged families also attend the school. The college has recently made some changes in its recruitment (though not admissions) policy to try to attract wealthier students on the grounds that it "increases economic diversity" (or possibly that they need more funding and would like to grant less financial aid), but this policy seems to be failing so far.

Minority Clubs
ASIA (Asian Students In Alliance)
ASU (African Students Union)
Chalutzim
Coalition of Anti-Racist Whites
Corean Student Union
ISO (International Student Organization)
LMNOP (Lesbian Movie Night: Organized Procrastination)
Native American Student Alliance
SOL (Student Organization of Latinas/Latinos)
Solidaridad
Stonewall Coalition

Students Speak Out On...
Diversity

"There is quite a large percentage of international students, but the socio-economic diversity seems to be on the decline."

Q "**Most of our minorities come from countries other than the US**. Economically, the school has been catering more to the upper-class, but the promise of meeting full need brings in more economically diverse people than peer schools. The campus is incredibly tolerant and obvious examples of prejudice are simply nonexistent."

Q "I would say campus is relatively diverse. I see a lot of international students when walking to class, but not a lot of the people I remembered from home. **There are not a lot of Muslims, and not a lot of inner-city blacks**. For instance, the free style contest was a huge letdown. No one could rhyme like my friends from Newark—no one. It made me miss home, but helped me to realize that I had arrived in the cornfields, for real now."

Q "Politically, there are many diverse ideas, though most of the ideas would be classified in the liberal spectrum. Socially, there are a lot of different ways people prefer to spend their time. Racially, there is more diversity at Grinnell than exists in Iowa on the whole, but the school is working to increase diversity on campus. Also, **there are quite a few international students on campus**."

Q "**Campus is not diverse yet**, but it is getting there!"

Q "**Grinnell is pretty diverse**. I know that I have not lacked for interracial or intercontinental friendship in my three years here."

Q "Socio-economically speaking, the campus is very diverse. **Racially, it's not that diverse**, but the college is much more diverse than its surroundings. The campus isn't that diverse politically in that the political scope of the campus generally ranges from liberal to extreme leftist. Additionally, there are a fair number of international students who add to our diversity. Also, the campus is quite diverse in terms of sexual orientation."

Q "Geographically, Grinnell is very diverse; there are a lot of international students, but they tend to hang among themselves. Grinnell tried to recruit more 'ethnic' students and faculty, but since both are self-selecting for the most part, **racial diversity is scant**."

Q "All the diversity makes this campus seem like an urban city in itself. The **liberality of the student body can make it seem closed-minded** to the conservative side."

Q "The campus could use more African-Americans, but for the middle of rural Iowa, I think that it's really pretty diverse. There are a lot of people who are not very rich who seem rich, and many more who you would assume to be dirt poor, but are rather well off. **There are diversity issues**, but the campus is very open, and there are many different types of people here. The smallest minority is either Morman (LDS) or republican."

The College Prowler Take On...
Diversity

According to Grinnell faculty, the percentage of minority students who go to Grinnell is comparable to other liberal arts institutions across the country. While it's true that most of the minority students at Grinnell are international students, the administration and a good majority of the student body is open to the idea of racial diversity on campus. Still, there is still only a small number of ethnic minorities on campus. This may be due to socio-economic reasons since Grinnell (like most private liberal arts colleges) is so expensive. However, there are many student groups for minorities that tend to be active on campus. Unfortunately, there have been reported incidents of racism in town. While this doesn't represent the attitude (or intelligence) of all the townies, as a rule they tend to be more closed-minded than college students and faculty.

Ideologically, it's not surprising that Grinnell is an overwhelmingly liberal institution. The faculty seems liberal enough (though in most classes, politics are taboo) and simply the liberal way that things are governed around campus is more acceptable to a leftist state of mind. There are a few conservative students who love Grinnell as much as any liberal, but it's likely that most right-wingers don't even consider Grinnell when filling out applications. The Campus Republicans probably have about six members, but occasionally they bring in controversial speakers like David Horowitz and company. In terms of acceptance of homosexuality, you can't do much better than Grinnell. Occasionally someone brings up the complaint that the gay, bisexual, and lesbian community doesn't stick together, but the counter-argument is that there's no need for them to stick together because everyone is fully accepting of them. Gay and straight people alike take full advantage of the Stonewall Resource Center, a facility that houses the headquarters of the Stonewall Coalition and a sizable library on topics relevant to the gay, bisexual, and lesbian community. Students at Grinnell are also accepting of sexual experimentation, which also eases the impact of coming out of the closet.

The College Prowler™ Grade on
Diversity: B-

A high grade in Diversity indicates that ethnic minorities and international students have a notable presence on campus and that students of different economic backgrounds, religious beliefs, and sexual preferences are well-represented.

Guys & Girls

The Lowdown On...
Guys & Girls

Men Undergrads:
45%

Women Undergrads:
55%

Birth Control Available?
Condoms are available at the Health Center and are given out free two at a time by friendly mom-like employees, but birth control prescriptions can be filled inexpensively at the Women's Health Center (717 5th Ave, Suite 4, 236-7787), along with other services such as STD testing. Morning after pills are available at the Health Center for $12.

Social Scene:
The student body at Grinnell tends to be friendly and accepting of pretty much anyone. It's easy to find a group of friends at the beginning of school, and there really are no cliques or social circles so, ultimately, it becomes easy to meet people

through friends. It's also relatively easy to simply bump into someone and start a conversation. This kind of interaction shortly becomes commonplace in a small college when you see the same people every day.

Hookups or Relationships?

Most of the students on campus seem to be more interested in hooking up with someone rather than actually dating them. While dating does happen on a regular basis, there is absolutely no pressure to have a boyfriend or girlfriend, and a lot of students would rather do without, so there are usually plenty of singles out on the weekend who want nothing more than a good fling.

Best Place to Meet Guys/Girls:

Typically, the best place to meet people of the opposite sex is wherever you happen to be hanging out. Guys and girls tend to hang out in the same social circles, and people usually get to know each other as friends before they begin dating or hooking up. Beyond that, Harris parties are renowned for being the place where hookups are as common as stalks in a cornfield. Hooking up at Grinnell is quite easy, that is if you can just work up the confidence level (or intoxication level) necessary to latch onto the dance partner of your choice.

Did You Know?
Top Places to Find Hotties:
1. Basketball Games
2. Burling
3. Mac Field on a spring day

Top Places to Hookup:
1. Harris Parties
2. The Pub
3. Burling 4th
4. The Forum pool hall
5. Younker Parties

→

Depending on whom you ask, either thirteen percent (officially) or sixty percent (according to most students) of Grinnell alumni marry other Grinnell Alumni?

There's a widely circulating rumor that Playboy magazine ranked Grinnell as having the least attractive student body?

An equally widely circulated rumor says that Playboy also ranked Grinnell's women as being more sexually satisfied than women at any other college in the country?

Dress Code

The Grinnell style of dress covers the entire spectrum, but it tends to be heavy on the peculiar or hippie side. Most students will simply go with a pair of scuffed up jeans that haven't been washed in a few days and a dingy T-shirt to match, but it's not uncommon to see designer bowler hats and camel-hair coats on guys or broomstick skirts and trench coats on girls. Nobody will give you a second glance as long as you have something on.

Students Speak Out On...
Guys & Girls

> "The guys and girls are super intelligent and cool. People here are very attractive, although not in a traditional way."

Q "The guys here tend to be varied; **there are a few jocks, but mostly geeks**. The women aren't terribly attractive, but that gets better once you realize that most students just most don't waste time on their appearance. The dating scene is pretty feminist, with both sexes being on pretty equal footing."

Q "Everyone gets **so used to each other here that no one bothers to dress up**, which gives Grinnellians a reputation for being ugly. Personally, I think that we're just comfortable with each other. For the most part, though, they are very accepting, wonderful people and after a while you stop caring that they're so, well, comfortable."

Q "The **girls are not super-model quality**, but many of them are attractive."

Q "**Everyone here is ugly**. I grew up in a rich neighborhood in New Jersey. The first thing I noticed when I arrived here was how ugly everyone was. If you are used to startlingly beautiful people, if you are from a high income neighborhood, yeah, you have to look past the skin, kids. I will wear things at college and walk around in them that I wouldn't be comfortable wearing in my own home."

Q "While there are some attractive individuals, Grinnell is **not the hottest school**, though guys are generally considered more attractive than the girls on the whole."

Q "Most students here are cute, but few are hot (If that makes any sense?). However, almost all students are interesting, intelligent, and able to hold up their end of a conversation. We all have some kind of quirk, but practically **everyone here is a nice, interesting person** if you take the time to get to know them. However, Grinnellians are in no way proud either."

Q "The **guys and girls at Grinnell are plain, weird**, and just plain weird. These kids are concerned more with changing the world than changing their looks."

Q "The students here are **hot, smart, and rich**—enjoy!"

Q "**Students here are artsy and, chances are, they're bi, gay, or lesbian**. I've started liking several girls only to find out that they were gay, and my current girlfriend is Bi. It just seems like it's a very prevalent trait. I suppose some of the guys are hot, but they're probably also gay. They're also probably the ones that bathe regularly. The opposite goes for the girls."

The College Prowler Take On...
Guys & Girls

Grinnell College students are rarely (conventionally) hot. While there are a few tan, thin blond girls and a handful of buff guys with chiseled features, clear skin, and carefully moussed hair, if you come to Grinnell looking for them specifically, you will be thoroughly disappointed. I hate to let you down, but few Grinnell girls even wear makeup, and some of the guys probably haven't showered or changed their clothes in about a week. Trust me, that ain't mousse, that's au naturale. And unless you're going to try to pick up some of the high-schoolers that drive around in circles on Saturday nights, you're pretty much stuck with the college options. However, if you're willing to look for something beyond what you see in a Calvin Klein commercial, you may find yourself very much in luck. Grinnell students are normally intelligent, socially concerned, fun-loving, friendly and kind individuals. How else do you think we all live together in a tiny college in a depressingly small town? Whether Grinnellians would look good on TV or not, they're at least capable of holding up a conversation after coming home to sum up an evening of drunken debauchery. Believe it or not, some people actually like the shaggy, rugged hippy, or adorable, quirky and befuddled look on guys, or girls who look spunky and unique instead of well-groomed and painted. If these sound like your type of people, you'll find no shortage of dream dates here.

That said, while finding a makeout buddy on a Saturday night is usually not that difficult, finding a girl or boyfriend might be. It's notoriously difficult to stay in a relationship at Grinnell. While nobody's exactly sure why it's so difficult to keep one dance partner here, it may have something to do with the general acceptability of making out with random people, or casual sex. Few people are ever called sluts here, either men or women, regardless of how comfortable they are with their sexuality. In fact, there is even a student group called Grinnellians Advocating Sexual Pleasure ("GASP") that encourages all kinds of safe sex, regardless of whether or not it's in a monogamous relationship. That freewheeling atmosphere probably puts a lot of strain on relationships, as does the unwieldy amount of academic stress most Grinnellians are saddled with. However, many students do get married to other Grinnellians after they graduate. Overall though, most students find the idea of marrying their classmates horribly, horribly spooky.

The College Prowler™ Grade on
Guys: B-

A high grade for Guys indicates that the male population on campus is attractive, smart, friendly, and engaging, and that the school has a decent ratio of guys to girls.

The College Prowler™ Grade on
Girls: B-

A high grade for Girls not only implies that the women on campus are attractive, smart, friendly, and engaging, but also that there is a fair ratio of girls to guys.

Athletics

The Lowdown On...
Athletics

Athletic Division:
Division III

Conference:
Midwest Athletic Conference

Men's Teams :
Cross Country
Soccer
Swimming
Basketball
Indoor Track
Outdoor Track
Baseball
Golf
Tennis
Football

Women's Teams:
Volleyball
Cross Country
Soccer
Golf
Tennis
Swimming
Basketball
Indoor Track
Outdoor Track
Softball

Club Sports:
Aikido
Baseball
Belly Dance
Dance
Disc Golf
Fencing
Field Hockey
Hacky Sack
Soccer
Juggling
Lacrosse (Men and Women's)
Marathon Running
Basketball
Ping Pong
Rugby
Tennis
Ultimate Frisbee (Men and Women's)
Water Polo
Volleyball
Wall Ball
Skateboarding

Number of Males Playing Varsity Sports:
218

% of Males Playing Varsity Sports:
34%

Number of Females Playing Varsity Sports:
190

% of Females Playing Varsity Sports:
23%

Athletic Fields

Rosenbloom Field
Springer Athletic Field
Ward Field
MacEachron Field
Les Duke Outdoor Track and Field
Oakland Acres Golf Course

School Mascot
The Pioneers

Getting Tickets
All sports events are free and open to everyone.

Most Popular Sports
Men's Basketball and Ultimate Frisbee

Overlooked Teams:
Men and Women's Track

Best Place to Take a Walk
The railroad tracks, Downtown, and The Grinnell Area Recreation Trail

Gyms/Facilities

The Physical Education Complex
The PEC has activities for just about everyone, including a weight room, climbing wall, indoor track, mat room, and racquetball court. It takes up a good chunk of the northeast campus for now, but a new one is being constructed to the North of Norris and Cowles on the very edge of the college.

Obermiller Swimming Pool
The swimming pool is located in the PEC. It's usually open until about 10 p.m. and is open to the public most of the time when the swimming or diving teams aren't practicing. The pool comes equipped with a good supply of toys, including fun noodles and kick boards.

Pfitsch Field House
This facility is also located in the PEC, and is the collective name for the building's 200m indoor track and weight room. It also includes facilities for all indoor track events.

Darby Gymnasium
The Darby Gym built in 1942 was torn down in the summer of 2004, but some of the bricks and the torches plaques that used to adorn the sides will be moved to a new "Darby" gym in the new Physical Education Complex. The gym was used primarily for basketball games.

Students Speak Out On...
Athletics

> "Grinnell is a Division III college, but we still take sports seriously. The intramural sports are pretty big as well. Intramural soccer is growing by the year!"

Q "I don't know anything about sports except our **basketball team rocks**."

Q "Lots of students play varsity sports; twenty-five percent I heard somewhere. Lots of **students pick up frisbee or soccer teams on their own**; it seems like everyone used to play something in high school. Sports games are not really well attended, except for basketball—everyone watches basketball here."

Q "As a Division III school, students who play varsity sports do so from the love of the game. **Intramurals are very popular** and are organized through talent levels rather than class rank."

Q "A fair number of people play varsity sports, but academics are top priority at Grinnell. Grinnell has a no-cut policy, though, so if you want to be on the team, you can be. You may not compete your first year, but you can become a part of the social network of the team. Intramurals **ultimate frisbee and rugby are particularly popular**."

Q "**People on the sports teams here think they are better than everyone else**, but I don't think anyone else cares."

Q "**Athletics here are not for the extremely competitive**. This is not the University of Iowa people!"

Q "Varsity sports? We have varsity sports? Oh, yeah; the people attending the games are one: the players and/or two: whoever the players cajoled into going to watch. The college is fiscally supportive, and has a number of good teams but, save for basketball, **no one gets too competitive**. Intramural sports are huge, though; ultimate frisbee and basketball are two Grinnell favorites."

Q "Grinnell is Division III, so **varsity sports are not that competitive**. Grinnell tends to have an unwritten 'no-cut' policy, which means that anyone who is willing to put in the work and effort to be on the team (and isn't a complete novice) is welcome to participate. This doesn't mean one will play in a game, but it's a great way to stay healthy and meet more people. IM sports are not as big yet, but they are growing in popularity."

Q "**Sports are much bigger than one might expect**; college wouldn't be the same without a select few dumb jocks."

The College Prowler Take On...
Athletics

Aside from basketball, athletics aren't a big deal at Grinnell. Even though a lot of people are on some team or another, few people who aren't friends with someone on the team show up to games. Sports teams try to advertise school sporting events as much as possible, but some Grinnell students would be hard-pressed to tell you where the outdoor track is. Also, the fact that we don't have any kind of stadium or outdoor arena doesn't help matters much. However, even with the often enforced athletic policy that absolutely anyone can play any sport without the fear of getting cut, all sports teams at Grinnell are not utterly horrible. All teams practice hard and play hard. Still, there's no denying that most students place athletics on the back-burner to make room for more studying and partying, two things that are essential in making up the Grinnell experience.

As mentioned above, the big exception to the lax athletic program at Grinnell is the men's basketball team. Basketball Coach David Arseneault has successfully implemented aggressive offensive playing strategies that lead to incredibly high-scoring games and consistent victories for the Pioneers! In fact, our team was featured in *ESPN: The Magazine* along with sections from Arseneault's newly released book called "The Running Game: A Formula for Success." Students love going to basketball games, most commonly with a liberal dose of alcohol in their system. The atmosphere at home games is totally insane! Suddenly, mild mannered economics majors become a part of a belligerent, jeering crowd. It's like Jekyll turned Hyde all over again! Grinnell students heckle the opposing team to the point that other schools shudder at the thought of having an away game scheduled in Darby Gymnasium. This kind of behavior has become a beloved tradition and shows no signs of stopping in the future. If you decide to go to the games there here are a few words of advice: be sure to wear red.

The College Prowler™ Grade on
Athletics: C+

A high grade in Athletics indicates that students have school spirit, that sports programs are respected, that games are well-attended, and that intramurals are a prominent part of student life.

Nightlife

The Lowdown On...
Nightlife

Bar Prowler: **Popular Nightlife Spots!**

The Pub
926 Main St.
Prices: $1.00-$1.75 draughts, $5.00-$7.00 pitchers, $1.50 shots, $1.75-$3.00 mixed drinks
Happy Hour: 4 p.m.-7 p.m. Fridays
This bar is essentially a Grinnell student hangout. There are available pool tables and a number of dart boards. They card, so don't count on getting in without an ID. While most students over 21 go here to have fun, there are rarely too many new faces from off campus.

Rabbit's
The corner of 4th and Main
Prices: $1.25 draughts, $2.00 bottles, $5.00 pitchers, $2.25-$3.00 mixed drinks
7 a.m. Happy Hour
This is more of a place for townies. Most of the patrons are middle-aged men, and the 7 a.m. happy hour caters to people who work the night

shift. However, you can go there to play computer games for a quarter a pop, which can seem like a pretty good option in a town without an arcade in sight. They also have quality pool tables at a price to match: $3.00 per hour. The bar also serves edible pizza, sandwiches, and chips.

John and Gary's Game Time
827 West St.

(641)236-4542

Prices: $1.00 draughts, $2.00-$2.75 mixed drinks

Happy Hour: 4-6 p.m.

This is basically your standard sports bar, complete with TVs tuned to whatever game is on. This bar caters more to the older townie crowd. In the way of beers, they serve Budweiser, Bud Light and Michelobe.

Bars Close At:
2 a.m.

Cheapest Place to Get a Drink:
The beer at Harris, and the admission for the parties there, is almost always free. Beyond that, drinks at the Pub and State Street are reasonably priced.

Student Favorites
The Pub, Harris Parties

Primary Areas with Nightlife:
Downtown

in dorms

in Harris

Local Specialties:
Student creations include "The Smelly Puto" (horchata and rum) and "The Camel Toe."

Useful Resources for Nightlife
The Campus Memo

Posters hung in the loggia

Word of mouth

What to Do if You're Not 21
All parties on campus are open to students of all ages, regardless of whether or not alcohol is being served. Also, Pagliai's usually doesn't card if you order a beer or two.

Organization Parties:

Almost all Harris parties are sponsored by various organizations, including the tennis team, National Jesus Incorporated, the Physics SEPC, EMANATE, etc, etc, etc. Occasionally a party will be held at an organization's headquarters, such as the BCC or Scarlet and Black.

Favorite Drinking Games:

Moose

Drunken Trivial Pursuit

Frats:

None

Students Speak Out On...
Nightlife

> "The parties on campus are quite excellent. Grinnell students party as hard as they work. There is one bar off-campus that is quite good also."

Q "One of the coolest things about parties at Grinnell is that they are open to anyone. You don't have to be a member of a particular frat or sports team to come. **There's usually a party at Harris** (an all-campus center, which houses dance parties and movies), a party in a dorm, and a party or two off-campus. In terms of bars, most people go to The Pub, which I gather is a rather relaxed place to hang out."

Q "**Parties are entirely on-campus**. Themed parties happen every week at the Harris Center and attract a decent crowd (they're also funded by the College)."

Q "I am not twenty-one, but **everyone goes to The Pub and State Street**. The Harris parties on campus are okay depending on the theme and DJ."

Q "**Parties on campus are free and open to everyone**. There are four lackluster bars in town, but most students choose to party on campus."

Q "**Harris parties are like going to a club except that you know everyone there**. So, some students avoid going at all costs. Other parties can be really fun. Birthday parties, music shows in gardener, all that is a good time—10-10 is awesome. My friends from Carleton come down just to be around for 10-10."

Q "The **only bar off-campus that I ever went to is called rabbits**—it's a chill place. Mostly old townie men hang out at Rabbits. They only serve at the bar, which is nice because if you're underage you can shoot pool and still hang out with your friends. Oh yeah, there's The Pub as well. It's this dingy underground place. They're really nice to you there, but you will need some government ID to get in; they throw college-focused parties, like '100 days' where everyone makes out."

Q "Parties on campus are a ton of fun. **Most dance parties are themed and all parties are open to everyone**. There are no cover fees, but students are expected to donate at each party. Some parties serve alcohol, but there is a wrist-band policy in which all students twenty-one and older receive wrist-bands. The favorite bar in town is The Pub and that's a pretty fun place too. The nice thing about Grinnell parties is that students watch out for one another and make sure they don't get themselves into trouble."

Q "Parties? Ha! **Don't come to school here if you're looking for wild parties**: or tame ones for that matter."

Q "**Everyone goes to The Pub or State Street on Wednesday nights**; students make sure to get MWF schedules just to make it convenient to go to The Pub on Wednesday nights and not have to wake up until Thursday afternoon. The parties on campus are awesome though, I could name several that were a highlight, 10-10, Alice in Wonderland, Relays, and especially Block Party (best time I ever had in my life was at block party this year). All the parties on campus are free. "

Q "**Parties on campus are pretty lame** compared to a state school, but they get the job done."

The College Prowler Take On...
Nightlife

Grinnell students tend to study hard and party hard. Basically every weekend there's at least one party going on, so drunken debauchery is never lacking here. The most well-known parties on campus are the Harris parties. A variety of school-based groups fund them, and students frequently find people at their doors with cups collecting for beer money. Most theme parties vary from creative to mundane, but a few annual favorites are sponsored by a particular group every year. These include the Underwear Ball, Halloween Masquerade Party, Fetish Party, and a cross-dressing party named after the Mary B. James dorms. They generally include loud pop and hip-hop music, lots of dancing, cool light effects, and copious amounts of free beer. Someone throws a Harris party almost every weekend and the administration has no problem with this.

Dorm parties at Grinnell, while less popular, also occur frequently. These are a lot like Harris parties, but they take place in some random residence hall and may or may not include loud music and lights. They almost always, however, include alcohol, and many cup-wielding organizers will show up at your dorm to beg for donations for these events as well. However, the beer at these parties tends to run out faster. There are only two bars in downtown Grinnell. The college favorite is The Pub, which is an underground bar downtown. Wednesday night drinking is an established pastime, and it's quite a popular place during finals week. The alcohol is relatively cheap, and seems to be of good quality. The Pub also has a policy of giving people $21 worth of free drinks on their twenty-first birthday. However, in the past few years they have begun to card students coming in. This is a big change from the previous policy, when anyone with a tad bit of facial hair could simply walk in and order anything. The newer State Street bar seems to be more lax now when it comes to underage drinking, but is also an establishment of lower quality. There is also a bar that tends to be open at all hours called The Rabbit, but it caters mainly toward town residents who work night jobs.

The College Prowler™ Grade on
Nightlife: B

A high grade in Nightlife indicates that there are many bars and clubs in the area that are easily accessible and affordable. Other determining factors include the number of options for the under-21 crowd and the prevalence of house parties.

Drug Scene

The Lowdown On...
Drug Scene

Most Prevalent Drugs on Campus:
Alcohol

Marijuana

Liquor-Related Arrests:
0

Drug-Related Arrests:
3

Drug Counseling Programs
Drug counseling is available from the Student Affairs staff. Professional help can be found at New Beginnings Recovery Center, 518 1st Ave, Newton, IA, 50208. Students whom the administration deem are in need of professional counseling are referred there.

Students Speak Out On...
Drug Scene

> "There's an active drug scene on campus regarding soft drugs (marijuana, LSD, mushrooms). Methamphetamines have invaded rural Iowa, but certainly not this school. Hard drugs are extremely rare and tend to be a private affair."

Q "There are **a lot of potheads** at Grinnell, but there's no pressure to become one. Alcohol is generally the preferred drug, but it gets pretty old pretty fast."

Q "There's **lots of pot on South campus**, but very little hardcore drug use goes on anywhere around campus."

Q "**Hard drugs (i.e. crack, cocaine, ecstasy) are rare**, but there are a lot of students on campus who smoke marijuana. However, there is never any pressure for a student to experiment with any drug. It's not like they're trying to sell students crack in the library."

Q "Grinnell is a very wet campus. **Alcohol is almost always prevalent at parties.** Weed is also present, and sometimes harder drugs rear their ugly heads at parties off-campus."

Q "There are drugs when students bring them back from Chicago or Minneapolis. Also, **some kids grow hallucinogenics**. Lots of people do drugs here and some people get busted. I would say about a third of the campus is stoned two-thirds of the time. There's even more drug use when marijuana has just arrived from a long dry spell."

Q "Weed is cheap in Iowa and s**ome people do Adderall to stay awake**. Other than that, no drugs are really available here. Some people do salvia, and occasionally there's a very small, but not very visible, group of people who experiment with more serious drugs (LSD or shrooms). Pot smoking is probably reaching about fifty percent of the campus though."

Q "**Drug use here is mostly recreational**. Alcohol and marijuana are the more prominent substances during the weekends."

Q "**You don't have to do drugs to have fun here**. However, if that's your thing, it's not hard to find the right people to hang out with."

The College Prowler Take On...
Drug Scene

The administration (and a large majority of the student body) believes that Grinnell has a drug problem. Within a few weeks, it becomes fairly obvious to new students that drinking heavily is the norm at Grinnell. Most first-years who come in believing that drinking will not affect their studies change their mind after the first semester or so. The college's alcohol policy is almost non-existent and many students abuse the lax policy. While students here, obviously, are not permitted to drink if they are underage, and, if of age, open containers are not tolerated on or around the vicinity of campus grounds under the college's policy of Self-Governance, these mandates are rarely enforced. Local police rarely get involved in school functions and will even make exceptions regarding underage and public drinking for events, such as the yearly outdoor Block Party. Wednesday night is also a traditional drinking night because many students have planned their schedule for the sole purpose of not having to attend classes on Tuesday or Thursday (or sleeping in). It seems that most theft and destruction of property that occurs on campus is done by people under the influence and, while it's fairly safe to leave your bike unlocked on a Monday, if left unguarded on a Friday night it's likely to be "confiscated" and crashed by a drunken reveler. Drunks also leave huge messes in residence hall lounges fairly often, and it's not uncommon for people to puke in hallways. Every few months an article will show up in the Scarlet and Black about some student being taken to the hospital for alcohol poisoning. This is usually the point at which the college will intervene and demand that the student seek professional help.

Marijuana is also commonly used by Grinnell students, but seems to have far less destructive effects. It seems that most people on campus have experimented with marijuana at some point. The college generally ignores it, despite the pungent odor that regularly wafts from one hallway to the next, but occasionally the local police do get involved. While warrants are almost never obtained merely for possession, once every one or two years, students are taken in on charges of possession with intent to sell. This can carry some heavy penalties, including up to several years of jail time. So far, though, most students arrested have been able to get off relatively light, and other students often pitch in to help pay for a lawyer. Hey, that's what friends are for.

The College Prowler™ Grade on
Drug Scene: C-

A high grade in the Drug Scene indicates that drugs are not a noticeable part of campus life; drug use is not visible, and no pressure to use them seems to exist.

Campus Strictness

The Lowdown On...
Campus Strictness

What Are You Most Likely to Get Caught Doing on Campus?

Spending too long in a 24-Hour parking zone

Smoking marijuana in a highly visible public place

Doing something really, unequivocally dumb and/or dangerous

Students Speak Out On...
Campus Strictness

"Campus police are very nice guys (the one female guard is wicked mean though). However, officers are required by law to report what they see. So don't let them see it."

Q "Policies are extremely lax in an official sense, with a strong emphasis on having students govern themselves. SAs monitor for habitual drug or alcohol (problem) users and those people get sent to rehabilitation. If you want to walk around and have a few beers or smoke a joint, absolutely no one will bother you. **Police presence on campus is very rare.**"

Q "**Security is not very strict here**. The college feels that its' students are responsible adults who are free to make their own decisions and mistakes."

Q "Grinnell exists under the auspices of self-governance, a policy which assumes students are adults and expects them to act as adults. Thus, students are expected to take care of themselves and each other. Rather than have outsiders enforce rules, **Grinnellians are content to self-regulate and act as a community**."

Q "**Campus Security is very lenient** about student drug use. The SAs here work as volunteers and nothing more."

Q "**We have an honor system**, so if you keep illegal substances in your room (or at least inside) you are pretty much safe from outside interference."

Q "The level of strictness here varies case by case. Usually, the college seems to have **a 'no harm, no foul' stance** that works very well. Besides, the work load here is so large that no student would dare risk getting too involved with drugs or alcohol because they'd do poorly in their classes. Most students are responsible and look out for others, but there's also a support system for those who need some help."

Q "**Authorities aren't strict at Grinnell**; self-governance ends up meaning that people are free to smoke up and drink in their rooms or lounges. There's not much done about illegal activity. Just don't let the town cops or the cleaning personnel see you."

Q "Lately the town police have been cracking down on drugs, but they remain **lax about alcohol**."

Q "**The administration is getting stricter**, which isn't saying much because they are pretty lenient."

The College Prowler Take On...
Campus Strictness

Thanks to Grinnell's policy of Self Governance, campus strictness is quite possibly among the most lenient of any college in the country. The Self Governance concept means that students are responsible for monitoring their own behavior and that of their fellow students. If you turn your music up too loud at 1 a.m. on a school night and you hear a knock on the door, you're definitely more likely to find your neighbor standing there than you are a ticked-off security guard. Self governance is, quite unanimously, Grinnell's most cherished policy. In 2004, when a security guard called the police on a few students for blatantly smoking marijuana in a school lounge, there was uproar on campus from students who claimed it was a direct violation of Self Governance. Many students even found it irrelevant that the students in question had been violating a national law. Self Governance was founded on the principle that only behavior that endangers other students is worthy of intervention by any outside force and students and faculty alike adhere to this.

Unfortunately, the Self Governance policy may not be permanent. The policy was created and upheld by Dean of Residence Life Steve Larson. Larson has since retired and the new Dean, Sherce Andrews, has stuck firmly by the policy, but there are no guarantees that his successor will continue the tradition. Occasionally, there are suggestions to have the policy made official in order to save it from one day being eliminated. So far, though, no one has taken much action. Another factor that contributes to the reigning benevolent anarchy on campus is the fact that rather than paid Resident Advisers, Grinnell has volunteer Student Advisers living on each floor. Since the SAs aren't paid, they don't don't feel overly obligated to report every unlawful incident that happens on their floor. In fact, SAs often drink and smoke right along with their first-years (oops, I let that one slip out).

The College Prowler™ Grade on

Campus Strictness: A-

A high Campus Strictness grade implies an overall lenient atmosphere; police and RAs are fairly tolerant, and the administration's rules are flexible.

Parking

The Lowdown On...
Parking

Approximate Parking Permit Cost
$50 per year

Grinnell Parking Services:
Security Office
1432 East St.
(641) 269-4600

Student Parking Lot?
Yes

Freshman Allowed to Park? Yes.

Parking Permits:
$50

Common Parking Tickets:
Failing to Register a Vehicle: $25
Not Having a Permit: $10
Expired Parking Meter: $10
No Parking Zone: $10
Handicapped Zone: $100
Fire Lane: $20

Did You Know?

Best Places to Find a Parking Spot
In the PEC

Good Luck Getting a Parking Spot Here:
In the parking lots behind the dorms

Students Speak Out On...
Parking

> "Yes, there is parking here. Sometimes, you might have to walk more than 100 feet, but there is parking available."

Q "It is **easy to park on campus**. Case closed."

Q "It's easy enough to park. Most people don't own cars and many tend to be filled, but a cheap parking pass will let you in ninety-nine percent of the time and otherwise, one might park a few blocks away. **Many students don't have cars** because, well, we're in the middle of nowhere."

Q "**Parking passes are cheap** but not rationed well, so sometimes finding a parking place can be difficult."

Q "Parking can definitely be a pain in the butt, but only if you are picky about parking somewhere near where you actually live. For more places to park, it is highly recommended that one purchase the **$50 parking permit that allows you to park in specially designated student lots** (which are sometimes full). Otherwise, you may be stuck with street parking, which is not entirely convenient."

Q "Yeah, **not too many people have cars here**, but most students here are friendly enough to let someone else borrow their car if they need it."

Q "**It's sometimes very difficult to find parking here**: Well, legal parking anyway."

Q "**I never have trouble parking**, but I live near south campus. I don't know about other areas. Also keep in mind that Grinnell is about to become a massive construction zone. So God only knows about the future of the Grinnell parking situation. Something tells me it's not at the top of His priority list."

The College Prowler Take On...
Parking

Few students on campus actually own cars. Except for traveling between cities, there's really no need for them. Even if you're going downtown when it's below zero degrees outside, in the time it takes you to walk to your car, get it started, navigate the icy roads around town, and find a parking space, you could already be warm and browsing through the menu inside Pagliai's. Even for those long road trips to Chicago, you can usually finagle some vehicle-owning sucker into going with you. This ultimately translates into limited demand for parking on campus. The parking lots near the dorms tend to be small, but instead of stretching a block away from your warm and cozy home, they're all right across the street. If these are full (and often they are), it's about another hundred feet to another parking lot outside the PEC that normally has plenty of available parking space.

However, there are some confusing parking regulations. Some of the parking lots, like the ones in front of the Admissions building, are only for faculty and visitors. There are also many 24-hour only parking spots located sporadically around campus, and students are frequently fined for leaving their cars there too long. Aside from these minor inconveniences however, students have little to no trouble at all finding a place to park on campus.

The College Prowler™ Grade on
Parking: B+

A high grade in this section indicates that parking is both available and affordable, and that parking enforcement isn't overly severe.

Transportation

The Lowdown On...
Transportation

Ways to Get Around Town
On Campus

You can use your feet or a bike. That's about it.

Public Transportation

Taxi Cabs
Courtesy Cab
(641) 236-4511
4 Washington Pl Grinnell
taxi50112@aol.com

Car Rentals

Alamo, local: (515) 256-5353
national: (800) 327-9633,
www.alamo.com

Avis, local: (515) 245- 2585
national: (800) 831-2847,
www.avis.com

Dollar, local: (515) 273-6100;
national: (800) 800-4000. www.dollar.com

Enterprise, local:(515)256-5665
national: (800) 736-8222,
www.enterprise.com

Hertz, local: (515) 285-9650
national: (800) 654-3131,
www.hertz.com

National, local: (515) 256-5353
national: (800) 227-7368,
www.nationalcar.com

Best Ways to Get Around Town

Your feet
A bike
Mooch a ride off a friend

Ways to Get Out of Town

Airport

Des Moines International Airport
(DSM) (515) 256-5100

Des Moines airport is probably the one most frequently used by Grinnell students. It's about an hour away by shuttle or a little less than an hour drive from the college.

Quad City International Airport
(MLI) (309) 764-9621

Quad City International Airport is about a 1-hour and 45-minute drive from Grinnell along I-80.

Airlines Serving Des Moines:

Allegiant Air, (702) 851-7300
www.allegiantair.com

American Airlines,
(800) 433-7300,
www.americanairlines.com

American Eagle,
(800) 443-7300,
www.aa.com

American West Express,
(800) 235-9292
www.americanwest.co

Continental Express,
(800) 523-3273,
www.continental.com

Chicago Express,
(800) 435-9282
www.chicagoexpress.com

Comair, (800)354-9822
www.fly-comair.com

Northwest, (800) 225-2525,
www.nwa.com

Mesaba Airlines,
(800) 225-2525
www.mesaba.com

Midwest Airlines
(800) 452-2022
www.midwestairlines.com

United, (800) 241-6522,
www.united.com

How to Get to the Airport

Grinnell security provides shuttles to and from Des Moines every break for about $10 per person. There are also a good number of people who live in Des Moines who you could probably bum a ride from.

Basically, you can get a ride from a friend or drive your own car.

Airlines Serving Cedar Rapids:

Allegiant Air, (702) 851-7300
www.allegiantair.com

American Airlines,
(800) 433-7300,

www.americanairlines.com
Delta, (800) 221-1212, www.delta-air.com
Northwest, (800) 225-2525, www.nwa.com
United, (800) 241-6522, www.ual.com

Airport
The Eastern Iowa Airport
2929 Wright Brothers Blvd W
Cedar Rapids, IA 52404
(319) 366-2246

The Eastern Iowa Airport is about 80 miles, or 1 hour 20 minutes driving time along I-80 East from Grinnell.

How to Get to the Airport
Airport Shuttle Service
2121 Wright Brother's Boulevard W
Cedar Rapids, IA, 52404
(319) 365-0655

Greyhound
www.greyhound.com
(800) 872-7245

While Greyhound has a stop in Grinnell, it does more have locations in Des Moines, Marshalltown, and Ames, all of which are within about an hour's driving time.

Amtrak
The closest Amtrak stop is Osceola, IA, which is about 100 miles away (an hour and a half, driving time). Call (800) 872-7245, or visit www.amtrak.com, for more information.

Travel Agents
Hamilton Travel LTD, 817 4th Ave Grinnell, (641)-236-3600

Tallyho Travel Tours and Cruises, 307 W. Main Marshalltown, (800) 359-5560

Students Speak Out On...
Transportation

> "I've heard the Greyhound stops in town, but Grinnell isn't big enough to warrant major transportation companies."

Q "**There is no public transit system**, but the town is small enough to be traversed by bike, foot, or snowmobile (if that's your thing). The campus Health Center does provide a shuttle to the hospital."

Q "**There's no public transportation in town**, but it's not like you need it—everything is within walking distance except the Wal-Mart."

Q "Just walk; there is no bus system, and if there was, it would have to go all of a half mile to get to the farthest place you'd need to go. Around breaks, **college security organizes shuttles to Des Moines international airport, and O'Hare in Chicago**."

Q "**There really isn't any form of public transportation here**. However, if you find an unlocked bike, it's yours to ride around on campus."

Q "Ha! Public transportation? **You mean walking, right?**

The College Prowler Take On...
Transportation

Currently, both on campus and in the town of Grinnell, there are no public transportation stops or facilities. There really isn't any need for them, since it takes about five to ten minutes to walk from one end of campus to the other, and twenty or thirty minutes to bike out of town. However, there are plans to revive the fondly-remembered but unsuccessful Campus Bikes program. These bikes used to be designated by a thin coat of orange spray paint. They were unlocked and were available for public use all over campus. Unfortunately, they were quickly trashed, but the campus has decided to bring them back using better, less fragile bikes.

As for transportation to and from Grinnell, Greyhound stops are not available in the town of Grinnell, but they are prevalent in Des Moines. However, most students who live more than a state away fly into the Des Moines airport and take the twenty-dollar-shuttle, courtesy of the security department, to Grinnell. Shuttles also go to and from the Minneapolis and Chicago airports each break for $40 and $45, respectively. If students have an emergency and need a ride out to the Des Moines airport in the middle of the year, arrangements can be made with the security department.

The College Prowler™ Grade on Transportation: D-

A high grade for Transportation indicates that campus buses, public buses, cabs, and rental cars are readily-available and affordable. Other determining factors include proximity to an airport and the necessity of transportation.

Weather

The Lowdown On...
Weather

Average Temperature
Fall: 60 °F
Winter: 20 °F
Spring: 60 °F
Summer: 80 °F

Average Precipitation
Fall: 3 in.
Winter: 1.2 in.
Spring: 3.5 in.
Summer: 4.3 in.

Students Speak Out On...
Weather

"All four seasons are present here, so be prepared for the very hot and the very cold. Iowa gets plenty of snow so bring, a coat, hat, boots, and a pair of mittens."

Q "Bring clothes—at least four sweaters. Also, pick out a hoodie that is a really good color for you and hides stains easily. You will want some sort of **winter jacket that is prepared for fifty and below**. It only gets that cold at night, though. However, you won't notice that it's that cold walking home from the pub, though. Note also: the ferocious wind is what really gets you in Iowa. A windproof jacket is a must during the winter."

Q "**It gets really cold in Iowa**, so come prepared. At the beginning and end of the school year, however, it is really hot and humid—definitely bring a fan!"

Q "We get both extremes here. It's very hot in August and September, and we get **negative wind chills in January**."

Q "**Summer, fall, and spring are gorgeous**; it is regularly shorts weather during these seasons. The winter can be pretty bitter and certainly takes some getting used to."

Q "Bring everything; it's 100 degrees in the summer (if you stay) and **negative forty in the winter**. Buying a good raincoat or windbreaker is the best purchase a student can make."

Q "It's sweltering hot for the first couple weeks, then it is freezing cold for the rest of the year. **Bring lots of coats, gloves, scarves, and winter hats.**"

> "The weather is schizophrenic in the summer and spring, and consistently cold in the winter. This **winter it was commonplace to have the daily high temperature below freezing**."

> "It gets cold in the winter; by cold I mean that **you will need a down jacket and one or two sweatshirts**. That said, it's never unbearable, and we're off school during winter break for the worst of the weather."

> "**Iowa weather is crazy**! You will need shorts and t-shirts for the beginning of the year and sweaters and jackets for the winter. Sometimes you'll need t-shirts for the winter and sweaters for the summer, however. I'm losing my mind!"

The College Prowler Take On...
Weather

The weather in Grinnell, as in most of the Midwest, can be downright schizophrenic. There are days in the winter where you can wear shorts and a t-shirt, and days in the middle of July when you'll need a heavy sweatshirt. We're like Mother Nature's little freak experiment. When you're packing to come back to Grinnell from a break, you may be stricken by the urge to leave all your clothes that are "out of season" at home. Do not surrender to this impulse! It's guaranteed that you'll regret it at least once or twice, probably many times more. The climate is not much better when the weather is in season. In the early fall when students arrive, the weather can be incredibly hot, and the soup-like humidity hanging in the air makes every last drop of sweat stick to your skin. On days when there's not even a breeze, wearing jeans and a long-sleeved t-shirt can make you miserably hot, and there's no air-conditioning in a lot of the dorms. Also, in the dorms that do have air conditioning, once they turn it on a drastic decrease in temperature outside can quickly make the air inside too cold for comfort. Grinnell is also in tornado alley, so you'll have to get used to the test runs of the tornado warning siren that are supposed to happen every Thursday at 9 a.m. in the spring and fall. The ear-piercing siren can sometimes be heard at random times, whether or not there's actually severe weather in the area.

In the winter, make sure to have your heaviest clothes handy, no matter how dorky they may look on you. The walk from your dorm to ARH can seem like an eternity when your face and neck go numb in the first few steps, so a scarf is worth it, no matter how fashionable it is. If you've never had your nose hairs freeze before, you will know what it feels like by the time you leave Grinnell. Between freezing and roasting however, there are some beautiful nights when you can sit out on the loggia under a clear sky and watch the stars, or spring days when there's nothing better than playing frisbee on Mac Field. If there's anything more beautiful in nature than Grinnell once the trees start to bloom, I have yet to see it. If anything, the Grinnell climate is perfect for the thousands of fireflies that take up residence on campus every summer.

The College Prowler™ Grade on

Weather: C+

A high Weather grade designates that temperatures are mild and rarely reach extremes, that the campus tends to be sunny rather than rainy, and that weather is fairly consistent rather than unpredictable.

GRINNELL COLLEGE
Report Card Summary

B+ ACADEMICS

C LOCAL ATMOSPHERE

A- SAFETY AND SECURITY

B+ COMPUTERS

B FACILITIES

D+ CAMPUS DINING

B- OFF-CAMPUS DINING

A- CAMPUS HOUSING

C+ OFF-CAMPUS HOUSING

B- DIVERSITY

B- GUYS

B- GIRLS

C+ ATHLETICS

B NIGHTLIFE

C- DRUG SCENE

A- CAMPUS STRICTNESS

B+ PARKING

D- TRANSPORTATION

C+ WEATHER

Overall Experience

Students Speak Out On...
Overall Experience

"My experience has been great! You'd be hard-pressed to find a school where more freedom is granted than Grinnell. The college really makes you feel alive!"

"My experience at Grinnell has been great. The **superior academics, the great party scene**, and the friendly townspeople are all irrelevant when you're surrounded by 1,300 inspired people all seemingly smarter than yourself. Here, I feel there's respect for intelligence and moreover, ingenuity. Frankly, I could've gotten the education I've received at Grinnell for the cost of a library card, but the enthusiasm that students and teachers exude comes only from one college: Grinnell."

Q "Grinnell is the only place I could see myself. **I love it here**. To quote 'Field of Dreams': 'Is this Heaven?' 'No, it's Iowa.'"

Q "I applied early decision to Grinnell, and I've never regretted that decision. However, **Grinnell is not for everyone**. Students here are given a lot of responsibility, and if a prospective student cannot handle responsibility well, they shouldn't apply. That also applies to students who are poor at handling stress because you will get stressed out at some point if you come to Grinnell. So, if you're a smart person who wants to meet some other fun kids, and you're not concerned about a good bit of work, then please apply because we'd love for you to come!"

Q "Grinnell is the perfect fit for me. My experience here has been made better by my peers and professors, both of whom invest heavily in what they do. **I wouldn't wish to be anywhere else**. Here I'm academically challenged in a non-competitive atmosphere. That's hard to come by in today's academia."

Q "Grinnell has its perks and jerks, but I wouldn't change schools for the world. I'm getting a great education and **I'm constantly meeting people who teach me about the world**. My peers are the men and women who really are going to make a difference someday."

Q "**I wouldn't trade Grinnell for the world**; it has been the best time of my life in every aspect. The people are first class, smart, nice, and enjoyable; you have to visit to meet the people here—trust me on the rest of what I've said."

Q "I love Grinnell—again, it's self-selected. If you want a big party school where it is possible to coast into a 3.0, Grinnell is not the school for you. If, however, you want **a tiny liberal arts college with tons of smart, friendly, albeit nerdy students**, you will love Grinnell. Students here are among the smartest, most accepting people I have ever met."

The College Prowler Take On...
Overall Experience

To be blunt, a vast majority of Grinnell students love it here. Students who choose to come here love the challenge they get from academia and their peers, and they love the amount of freedom that the administration gives them (mostly through Self Governance). Grinnell students are free to learn and grow into responsible, conscientious adults, and the students here are thankful that the school they've chosen has given them the opportunity to thrive. Some students can't even imagine what it would be like if they'd ended up somewhere else.

Yeah, Grinnell students complain sometimes about the things that aren't available to them that would be at their disposal at a larger, city school. We gripe about excess construction, bogus administration policies, and the things that fellow Grinnellians do that just plain bug us. Overall though, most of the students here are happy with the decisions they've made and the direction they're going in their lives, and a lot of them have the Grinnell faculty, students, and townspeople to thank for that. Although living in rural Iowa does take some getting used to (especially if you're from out-of-state), most students don't mind making Grinnell their home for four years. Despite the schizophrenic weather, lackluster athletic program, sub-par dining hall food, and the immature townies; many students have taken comfort in the fact that it's "just us" here amongst the cornstalks. When a Grinnell graduate thinks back upon his or her Grinnell experience and all the fond memories that come along with it, everything else seems like small potatoes.

The Inside Scoop

The Lowdown On...
The Inside Scoop

Grinnell Slang

Know the slang, know the school. The following is a list of things you really need to know before coming to Grinnell. The more of these words you know, the better off you'll be.

Pit: The basement level of a residence hall

Stalker Net: The Grinnell Online Directory

RKO: Russel K. Osgood, the current president of the college

Prospie: A prospective student

Sex: Southern Express

Hell Week: The week before finals, when papers and other assignments are due for most classes.

Hookup: Generally taken to mean a one-night session full of anything from making out to, but not including, sex.

Beach: The area in front of a dorm (Norris "Beach" is the courtyard in front of Norris) Hey, we're in Iowa. We have to substitute for the real thing.

Fac Man: Facilities Management

Plancrastination: Procrastinating by checking or updating Plans

No Love: "You have failed"

Sketchy: Of questionable morals

Leiny's: Leinenkugel's beer, a Grinnell favorite

Things I Wish I Knew Before Coming to Grinnell

- No matter how smart you are, there will be a lot of people here who are smarter than you.
- The departments can be picky about which AP and IB credits you can actually use to skip prerequisites or count for your major.
- Don't be afraid to talk to the professors.
- If you really, really need an extension, ask for it.
- Make friends with the people on your floor—they're the most convenient people to go to for a sympathetic ear or pester when you're procrastinating.
- Bring a bike.
- The workload can be killer.

Tips to Succeed at Grinnell

- Turn in all your papers (even if they're excessively late).
- Do the reading—at least before the final.
- Study for the finals. They can be worth about a third of your grade sometimes.
- Find people to study and work with, especially for math and science.
- Ask your professors for help when you don't understand something.
- Try to show up for class, especially if participation is a part of your grade.
- As hard as it is, try not to procrastinate. This will save your life during Hell Week.
- Take classes you think you'll actually enjoy.

Grinnell Urban Legends

- Over 60% of Grinnell alumni marry other Grinnell alumni.
- Playboy ranked Grinnell No. 1 Ugliest Student Body in America.
- Playboy also ranked Grinnell's women as Most Sexually Satisfied among college students in America.
- Students can be expelled for grabbing onto the side of one of the slow-moving trains that go through campus.

School Spirit

School spirit at Grinnell isn't a very visible phenomenon. You won't find any cheerleading or pep squads here. There are no Grinnell College parades, and the sports teams are a peripheral anomaly regarding campus life. If you ask a Grinnellian about some aspects of the college like dining or diversity, they're liable to give you a pretty negative response, and sometimes all that complaining can give people the wrong idea. But if you ask a Grinnellian whether or not they like it here, almost all of them will tell you how much they adore their school. Make no mistake about it, the students who go here are Grinnellians for life, and they wouldn't have it any other way.

Traditions

Spring and Winter Waltz

These are the two formal dances at Grinnell that take place, as the name suggests, every winter and spring. The dress code is very formal. Men wear tuxes or suits and women wear dresses fit for Prom night. High-class pre-parties with fancy foods are the norm, and most people get a bit drunk before hitting the dance floor in front of a live jazz band. Sometimes campus groups host a dance class before the waltz so people actually know what to do when the waltzing music starts. Normally, students end up looking like fools, but it's a blast all the same.

Two a.m. Bakery Run

On weeknights the Danish Maid Bakery finishes baking it's pastries at 2 o'clock in the morning. If you're up late studying (or doing anything else for that matter), it's traditional to take a quick run downtown to get something fresh out of the oven.

Relays

This late spring event is something of a spoof on the Olympics, complete with a faculty-lit flaming toilet bowl to kick off the games. The ensuing events are basically beer sports, including keg stands and the like. Recently the administration decreed that the beer used must be non-alcoholic, but while the beverage in the games may be O'Douls, the beer kegs in nearby residence halls are anything but.

Titular Head

Near the end of the school year, Grinnell hosts a spoof film festival where students submit movies that run under five minutes. Tickets always disappear early, but it is fairly simple to make fake ones using the right kind of paper and a high-quality copy machine (don't ask me how I know this). A panel of judges hands out zany-looking trophies to the best films, and a series of prank awards for all the runners-up. The event has spawned campus classics such as "Racquetball Tunak Tunak Tun," which follows a racquetball game set to the title song all over campus, and "Burling: I Do It All The Time," a music video for the Violent Femmes song "Kiss Off" set in Burling library, both of which are available on Phynd.

100 Days

A hundred days before graduation, The Pub throws a party for all seniors, the main purpose of which is for all the soon-to-be-departing Grinnellians to make out with all of the people they've had the hots for since Freshman year. A plentiful amount of alcohol is, of course, involved.

Block Party

On the last day of finals, a sizable chunk of High Street is blocked off from early in the afternoon until early evening. A beer truck is pulled in, a live campus band strikes up, and couches, tables, and chairs are hauled out into the street. Normally, the cops look the other way, and everyone parties like there's no tomorrow. Most students say the main purpose of Block Party is to get extremely drunk, but on a nice summer day after you've won your freedom from a hard school, sitting out in the sun with a bunch of friends is fun any way you look at it.

One Acts

One Acts is a theatre tradition on campus that has been going on for years. These short plays are student directed and acted, and each lasts for about fifteen minutes to half-an-hour. They're usually played in The Wall theatre in Bucksbaum for two nights, and, like most plays, they sell out quickly, so get a ticket early. The types of plays range from conventional to extremely experimental. Some are actually student-written.

The Salon

Around Finals, a student art show is held in Faulconer Gallery. All students can submit works, and a professional artist judges the pieces and decides which ones to include in the show. The judge also decides which piece is the best in the show. Two runners-up are also named.

Burling 4th Bathroom

It's a tradition to scrawl graffiti on the walls of the bathroom on Burling 4th. Some of the scribbles are profound, and some are petty, but it does contribute to the unique place that the most remote corner of the library holds in many Grinnellian's hearts. The Burling 4th Bathroom also has a reputation for being the location of many scandalous encounters.

Moose

By far the most popular drinking game at Grinnell, this beloved sport involves an ice cube tray, a quarter, and a whole lot of beer. The ice cube tray is set up in a line away from the person whose turn it is with a full beer cup directly behind it. The idea is to bounce the quarter into the ice cube tray. If you succeed in getting it in the tray, count how many ice cubes away from the front the quarter landed; this represents the number of chugs of beer involved. If the quarter lands on the right side of the tray, you select one other person playing the game to take that many chugs. If it lands on the left side, you drink that many chugs of beer. If the quarter lands in the last two cube compartments, everyone has to put their hands up next to their head (moose-antler style) and scream "Moose!" The last person who does this has to drink the whole cup of beer (known as the "Moose Cup." If the person playing gets the quarter into the cup, he or she has to drink the Moose Cup. The tray moves on to the next person as soon as the person playing misses. Most students are introduced to this game their freshman year.

Alice

The traditional outdoor Alice party began in 1980, died out in the nineties, and has recently been revived. The main point of Alice is to get as "trippy" as possible, in the literal, hallucinogenic sense of the word. While not everyone at Alice is actually tripping, the party focuses on activities that could be really cool in an altered state, like making tie-dye shirts and mixing a giant batch of home-made playdough in a kiddie pool.

Finding a Job or Internship

The Lowdown On...
Finding a Job or Internship

Finding a job in Grinnell isn't difficult. It's fairly easy to find campus employment, whether it be in the dining halls (where most work-study students end up), the newspaper, or as a lab assistant. The only real problem with working for the college is that the hours tend to be short because so many students are trying to pay their way, but there's simply not enough work to go around. Finding a job in town can be slightly more difficult, but between the local restaurants and video rental stores, if one can effectively compete with high school students, jobs are available.

While there aren't many internships available on campus, the Career Development Office has listings of many different internships that students can take advantage of during the summer. The college funds some internships that are exclusively for Grinnell students to the tune of a few thousand dollars. Also, if students can find other internships, Grinnell will often pay students a stipend for them.

Advice

Most Grinnell students take the opportunity to do an internship or summer scientific research at some point in their college careers. There are always people in the Career Development Office who would love to do everything they can to help you score the perfect job, before or after graduation. Just keep your eyes and ears open for announcements.

Career Center Resources & Services

Advertises local jobs
Coordinates internships
Funds about a dozen different internships for Grinnellians only each summer
Career workshops
Offers graduate school information
Brings recruiters to campus

Local Employment Agencies:

Manpower Inc.
808 5th Ave. Grinnell
641-236-5528

Workforce Development
123 6th Ave Grinnell
641-236-4732

Graduates Who Enter Job Market within 1 Year of Graduation:

20%

Alumni

The Lowdown On...
Alumni

Website:
http://www.grinnell.edu/alumni/

Office:
Office of Alumni Relations and Development
733 Broad St.
Grinnell, IA, 50112
(641) 269-3206
(800) 241-5084
(641) 269-4313 (Fax)

Services Available
Alumni directory
Help finding employment

Major Alumni Events

The biggest alumni event is, of course, the reunion held at the college every summer, where alums stay in their old dorms, revisit their old stomping grounds, and reminisce about that time that so-and-so jumped off a second story landing while completely plastered. The college also sponsors Alumni travel programs across the globe and organizes local potlucks for Grinnell graduates.

Alumni Publications

Grinnell Magazine

Did You Know?

Many Grinnellians who have graduated in the past few years still keep in touch with the college community through Plans.

Famous Grinnell Alums—

Kevin Cannon (Class of '02) Comic strip artist

Emily Bergl (Class of '97) Star of Carrie 2 and Broadway productions

Amy Johnson (Class of '85) Opera singer

Thomas Cech, (Class of '70), Co-recipient of the 1989 Nobel Prize in chemistry and president of the Howard Hughes Medical Institute

John Garang (born John Mabior) (class of '69) Leader of the Sudan People's Liberation Army rebel forces.

Robert Noyce (Class of '49) Co-inventor of the integrated circuit and co-founder of Intel.

Gary Cooper (Class of '26) Oscar-winning actor

Student Organizations

Academic Team -quizbowl@grinnell.edu
Ace Bomb! - abebomb@grinnell.edu
ACLU - aclu@grinnell.edu
Alpine Club – alpine@grinnell.edu
Alternative Break – altbrk@grinnell.edu
Alternate Happy Hour – ahh@grinnell.edu
Amnesty International – amnesty@grinnell.edu
Anglers Association of Grinnell
Anime – http://web.grinnell.edu/groups/anime/ anime@grinnell.edu
Anti-War Alliance – http://www.grinnell.edu/student/groups/antiwar/ antiwar@grinnell.edu
ASIA (Asian Students in Alliance) – http://web.grinnell.edu/groups/asia/ asia@grinnell.edu
ASU (African Students Union)
B & S – fakepapr@grinnell.edu
Backtable – them@grinnell.edu
Baseball Club – baseball@grinnell.edu
Beard and Moustache Society – gbams@grinnell.edu
Belligerency Club – belliger@grinnell.edu

Belly Dance – belly@grinnell.edu
Billiards Club – billiard@grinnell.edu
BLAH (The Computer Games Group)- blah@grinnell.edu
Boggle Club – bogglers@grinnell.edu
Bridge Club – bridge@grinnell.edu
Buddies (Davis Elementary School) -buddies@grinnell.edu
Burnt Lemon Cake Fan Club
Campus Democrats – democrat@grinnell.edu
Canterbury Club – cntrbry@grinnell.edu
CBS (Concerned Black Students – http://www.grinnell.edu/student/groups/cbs/
cbs@grinnell.edu
Chalutzim – chalutz@grinnell.edu
Chess Club – chess@grinnell.edu
Chips 'N Dip – chipndip@grinnell.edu
Coalition of Anti-Racist Whites – http://www.grinnell.edu/student/groups/carw/   carw@grinnell.edu
College Republicans – http://web.grinnell.edu/groups/republic/
republic@grinnell.edu
Con Brio – http://web.grinnell.edu/groups/conbrio/
conbrio@grinnell.edu
Conflict Resolution Group – http://www.grinnell.edu/student/groups/crg/
crg@grinnell.edu
Corean Student Union – http://web.grinnell.edu/groups/corea/
corea@grinnell.edu
CND – cnd@grinnell.edu
Crocheting and Knitting Coalition – cakc@grinnell.edu
Dagorhir – sword@grinnell.edu
Dance, Dance, Revolution – ddr@grinnell.edu
Dance Team – dance@grinnell.edu
Dialogues in Christianity – dialogue@grinnell.edu
Disc Golf Club
DRAW (Develop Raw Artist Within) – draw@grinnell.edu
EAG (Environmental Action Group) – http://web.grinnell.edu/groups/eag/
eag@grinnell.edu
EMANATE! - emanate@grinnell.edu
Europa – europa@grinnell.edu
EXCO (Experimental College) – exco@grinnell.edu
EZ News – eznews@grinnell.edu
FAC (Feminist Action Coalition) – fac@grinnell.edu
Field Hockey – fhockey@grinnell.edu

FIMRC (Foundation for the International Medical Relief of Children)
FNORD (Grinnellians in Favor of Discord) – fnord@grinnell.edu
Freesound – http://web.grinnell.edu/groups/freesound/ freesoun@grinnell.edu
FTP (Free the Planet) – http://web.grinnell.edu/groups/FTPlanet/ ftplanet@grinnell.edu
G-Tones (Male Acapella Group) – gtones@grinnell.edu
Gamers' Guild – gamers@grinnell.edu
GASP (Grinnellians Advocating Sexual Pleasure) -gasp@grinnell.edu
Gathering – cardgame@grinnell.edu
GIMP (Grinnell Independent Musical Productions) gimp@grinnell.edu
Grinnell College Christian Fellowship – gccf@grinnell.ed
Grinnell Community Action Network – gcan@grinnell.edu
Grinnell GO Club – goclub@grinnell.edu
Grinnell Independent Theatre
Grinnell Students for Dean – deanin04@grinnell.edu
Grinnell Wussie Punchers – wusspnch@grinnell.edu
Grinnellians for Economic and Social Diversity – gesd@grinnell.edu
Grinnellians for Gephardt
Grinnellians on Religious Dialogue- god@grinnell.edu
GSAS (Grinnell Students against Scurvy) – scurvy@grinnell.edu
GUMBO (Grinnell United Mountain Bike Org.) - gumbo@grinnell.edu
Habitat for Humanity – habitat@grinnell.edu
Hacky Sack Club – hackeysac@grinnell.edu
Happy New Year Club
Healthy Body and Healthy Mind – bhealthy@grinnell.edu
HOTSQUAT – hotsquat@grinnell.edu
Interior Design Group
International Soccer Club I
International Soccer Club II – soccer@grinnell.edu
International Speakers Program – isp@grinnell.edu
ISO (International Student Organization) – http://web.grinnell.edu/groups/iso/ iso@grinnell.edu
Juggling – juggling@grinnell.edu
Just Sex (Sexual Assault Working Group) – justsex@grinnell.edu
Kid's Art – kidsart@grinnell.edu
Lacrosse- Men's – guyslax@grinell.edu
Lacrosse – Women's – lax@grinnell.edu
Leaf – lan@grinnell.edu
Lifeguards – guard@grinnell.edu
Link – Grinnell Whitehat Hacking Club – link@grinnell.edu
LMNOP (Lesbian Movie Night;

Organized Procrastination) – lmnop@grinnell.edu
LUSH
Maple Leaf Amalgamation (MLA) – canada@grinnell.edu
Marathon Club
Meditation Group – meditate@grinnell.ed
MIDSG (Mental Illness Discussion and Support Group) – midsg@grinnell.edu
Ministry of Design – mod@grinnell.edu
Mock Trial Association – mock@grinnell.edu
Model UN – modelun@grinnell.edu
Mountaineering Club – climb@grinnell.edu
National Jesus Incorporated – jesus@grinnell.edu
Native American Student Alliance – nasa@grinnell.edu
NBA Basketball Club
ODISI (Open Dialogue on Issues of Social Inequality) – odisi@grinnell.edu
Pagan Discussion Circle – http://web.grinnell.edu/groups/pagan/ pdc@grinnell.edu
PAN (Poverty Action Now) – homeless@grinnell.edu
Paragon – paragon@grinnell.edu
PBS (Pitt Barbecue Society)
Photo Society
Ping Pong – pingpong@grinnell.edu
Poker Club
Potty Poetry Coalition – ppc@grinnell.edu
Prison Writer's Workshop – prison@grinnell.edu
Quaker – quaker@grinnell.edu
Radical Cheerleaders – cheer@grinnell.edu
RAW Club – rawclub@grinnell.edu
Red Cross – redcross@grinnell.edu
Relays – relays@grinnell.edu
Ritalin Test Squad – improv@grinnell.edu
Rocky Horror Picture Show – rocky@grinnell.edu
Rugby -Men's and Women's – wrugby@grinnell.edu
S & B (Scarlet and Black) – newspapr@grinnell.edu
SACC (Student Academic Computer Committee) – sacc@grinnell.edu
SCA (Society for Creative Anacronism) – http://web.grinnell.edu/groups/sca/
sca@grinnell.edu
Sex E Men – sexemen@grinnell.edu
ShaW (Student Health and Wellness Committee) – schealth@grinnell.edu

Social Justice Action Group – sjag@grinnell.edu

Society for Fiction and Fantasy – scifi@grinnell.edu

SOL (Student Organization of Latinas/Latinos) – sol@grinnell.edu

Solidaridad (Latin American Solidarity Group) – americas@grinnell.edu

Sporting Wood: Carpentry Club

Stonewall Coaltion – stoneco@grinnell.edu

Student Alumni Association – saa@grinnell.edu

Student Campaign for Increased Political Engagement (SCIPE) – politics@grinnell.edu

Student Endowment Investment Group – invest@grinnell.edu

Students Against Sweatshops – http://web.grinnell.edu/groups/nosweat/ nosweat@grinnell.edu

Students for International Democracy – sid@grinnell.edu

Students for John Kerry for President

Techno Club – technoclub@grinnell.edu

Tennis Team

Terpsichore – tchore @grinnell.edu

Titular Head – titular@grinnell.edu

Turkish Belly Dance@grinnell.edu

Ultimate Frisbee, Men – frisbee@grinnell.edu

Ultimate Frisbee, Women – stickies@grinnell.edu

Unitarian Universalist Campus Group – uu@grinnell.edu

Vegan Coop – vegcoop@grinnell.edu

VISA (Volunteers in Student Admission) – visa@grinnell.edu

Volleyball Club – volleyball@grinnell.edu

VOX – voxy@grinnell.edu

Wall Ball Club – wbl@grinnell.edu

We Are – weare@grinnell.edu

Wheels of Steel

4 Elements – 4element@grinnell.edu

The Best & The Worst

The Ten BEST Things About Grinnell:

1. Amazing and Caring Professors
2. Titular Head
3. Phynd
4. Waltz
5. Block Party
6. Sexual Promiscuity
7. Bob's Underground
8. Harris Parties
9. Unabashed Individuality
10. Trees on campus blooming in Spring

The Ten WORST Things About Grinnell:

1. Poor Dining Hall Food
2. Rude High School Townies
3. Long, Cold Winters
4. Walking to Class in the middle of Winter
5. Social Claustrophobia
6. Immature Drunks on Weekends
7. Smoky Lounges
8. The Heavy Workload
9. Way too many Students with Depression
10. Geographical Isolation

Visiting Grinnell

The Lowdown On...
Visiting Grinnell

Hotel Information

Cafe Phoenix and Inn
http://www.thephoenixcafe.com/
834 Park St
Grinnell, IA 50112
(641) 236-3657
Price Range: $55-$65

Carriage House Bed and Breakfast
1133 Broad St.
Grinnell, IA 50112
(641) 236-7520
Price Range: $60-$80

Clayton Farms Bed and Breakfast
621 Newburg Road
Grinnell, IA 50112
(641) 236-3011

Country Inn
http://www.countryinns.com/grinnellia
Hwy 146 north of I-80
Grinnell, IA 50112
(641) 236-9600
Price Range: $70 - $90

Days Inn
Hwy 146 north of I-80
Grinnell, IA 50112
(641) 236-6710
Price Range: $48- $75

Guest House Bed and Breakfast
http://www.ia-bednbreakfast-inns.com/guesthouse.htm
3974 50th St
Grinnell, IA 50112
(641) 236-0132
Price Range: $65-$85

Marsh House Bed and Breakfast
http://www.ia-bednbreakfast-inns.com/marshhouse.htm
833 East St
Grinnell, IA 50112
(641) 236-0132
Price Range: $65-$79

Super 8
Hwy 146 north of I-80
Grinnell, IA 50112
(641) 236-7888
Price Range: $40-$55

To Schedule a Group Information Session or Interview:

Summer:
Monday through Friday, 11:30 a.m. and 2:30 p.m.

Fall:
Monday through Friday 9:00 a.m., 10:00 a.m., 11:00 a.m., 1:00 p.m., 2:00 p.m. and 3:00 p.m., Saturday: 9:00 a.m., 10:00 a.m. and 11:00 a.m.

Interviews:

Summer:
Monday through Friday, 9:00 a.m., 10:00 a.m., 1:30 p.m. and 2:30 p.m.

Fall:
Monday through Friday 9:00 a.m., 10:00 a.m., 11:00 a.m., 1:00 p.m., 2:00 p.m., and 3:00 p.m., Saturday: 9:00 a.m., 10:00 a.m., and 11:00 a.m.

Campus Tours
Summer:

Monday through Friday, 8:30 a.m., 10:00 a.m., 1:00 p.m. and 2:30 p.m.

Fall:

Monday through Friday 9:00 a.m., 10:00 a.m., 11:00 a.m., 1:00 p.m., 2:00 p.m., and 3:00 p.m., Saturday: 9:00 a.m., 10:00 a.m., and 11:00 a.m.

Overnight Visits:

High school seniors, and occasionally juniors, frequently stay for one or two days with Grinnell students as "Prospies," or Prospective Students. While juniors are only allowed to stay between Sunday and Thursday night, seniors often stay over on or near a weekend to get a taste of the recreational and social endeavors at Grinnell. Most Grinnellians love prospies, or more specifically, corrupting prospies. Really, most prospie hosts just want to share what they love about Grinnell with high school students to convince them to come here. Students will almost always find something for their prospies to do, like go to plays or parties and play pool, and introduce them to as many other Grinnell students as they possibly can. During the day, most visitors sit in on one or two classes that catch their eye, attend informational meetings, and talk to faculty members from departments the students take an interest in. Many prospies who decide to come to Grinnell look for their hosts from the year before as soon as they arrive on campus. A lot of Grinnell students say that their prospie visit was a blast and convinced them to enroll, but some students find out after living for a few days on campus that Grinnell just isn't for them.

To set up a visit, contact the Admissions Office

(800) 247-0113

(641) 269-3600

askgrin@grinnell.edu

Directions to Campus

Driving from the North
Take I-35 South

Merge into I-235 S via the left exit to Des Moines

Merge onto I-80 E via exit 87A toward Davenport

Take the IA-146 exit (number 182) toward Grinnell and New Sharon

Turn left on IA-146 N.

Turn right onto Hwy. 6

Turn into the admissions parking lot.

Driving from the South
Take I-35 N

Stay straight to go onto I-80 E

Take the IA-146 exit (number 182) toward Grinnell and New Sharon

Turn left on IA-146 N.

Turn right onto Hwy. 6

Turn into the admissions parking lot.

Driving from the East
Take I-80 W

Take the IA-146 exit (number 182) toward Grinnell and New Sharon

Turn right on IA-146 N.

Turn right onto Hwy. 6

Turn into the admissions parking lot.

Driving from the West
Take I-80 E

Take the IA-146 exit (number 182) toward Grinnell and New Sharon

Turn left on IA-146 N.

Turn right onto Hwy. 6

Turn into the admissions parking lot.

Words to Know

Academic Probation – A student can receive this if they fail to keep up with their school's academic minimums. Those who are unable to improve their grades after receiving this warning can possibly face dismissal.

Beer Pong / Beirut – A drinking game with numerous cups of beer arranged in a particular pattern on each side of a table. The goal is to get a ping pong ball into one of the opponent's cups by throwing the ball or hitting it with a paddle. If the ball lands in a cup, the opponent is required to drink the beer.

Bid – An invitation from a fraternity or sorority to pledge their specific house.

Blue-Light Phone – Brightly-colored phone posts with a blue light bulb on top. These phones exist for security purposes and are located at various outside locations around most campuses. If a student has an emergency or is feeling endangered, they can pick up one of these phones (free of charge) to connect with campus police or an escort service.

Campus Police – Policemen who are specifically assigned to a given institution. Campus police are not regular city officers; they are employed by the university in a full-time capacity.

Club Sports – A level of sports that falls somewhere between varsity and intramural. If a student is unable to commit to a varsity team but has a lot of passion for athletics, a club sport could be a better, less intense option. If a club sport still requires too much commitment, intramurals often involve no traveling and a lot less time.

Cocaine – An illegal drug. Also known as "coke" or "blow," cocaine often resembles a white crystalline or powdery substance. It is highly addictive and dangerous.

Common Application – An application that students can use to apply to multiple schools.

Course Registration – The time when a student selects what courses they would like for the upcoming quarter or semester. Prior to registration, it is best to have an idea of several back-up courses in case a particular class becomes full. If a course is full, a student can place themselves on the waitlist, although this still does not guarantee entry.

Division Athletics – Athletics range from Division I to Division III. Division IA is the most competitive, while Division III is considered to be the least competitive.

Dorm – Short for dormitory, a dorm is an on-campus housing facility. Dorms can provide a range of options from suite-style rooms to more communal options that include shared bathrooms. Most first-year students live in dorms. Some upperclassmen who wish to stay on campus also choose this option.

Early Action – A way to apply to a school and get an early acceptance response without a binding commitment. This is a system that is becoming less and less available.

Early Decision – An option that students should use only if they are positive that a place is their dream school. If a student applies to a school using the early decision option and is admitted, they are required and bound to attend that university. Admission rates are usually higher with early decision students because the school knows that a student is making them their first choice.

Ecstasy – An illegal drug. Also known as "E" or "X," ecstasy looks like a pill and most resembles an aspirin. Considered a party drug, ecstasy is very dangerous and can be deadly.

Ethernet – An extremely fast internet connection that is usually available in most university-owned residence halls. To use an Ethernet connection properly, a student will need a network card and cable for their computer.

Fake ID – A counterfeit identification card that contains false information. Most commonly, students get fake IDs and change their birthdates so that they appear to be older than 21 (of legal drinking age). Even though it is illegal, many college students have fake IDs in hopes of purchasing alcohol or getting into bars.

Frosh – Slang for "freshmen."

Hazing – Initiation rituals that must be completed for membership into some fraternities or sororities. Numerous universities have outlawed hazing due to its degrading or dangerous requirements.

Sports (IMs) – A popular, and usually free, student activity where students create teams and compete against other groups for fun. These sports vary in competitiveness and can include a range of activities—everything from billiards to water polo. IM sports are a great way to meet people with similar interests.

Keg – Officially called a half barrel, a keg contains roughly 200 12-ounce servings of beer and is often found at college parties.

LSD – An illegal drug. Also known as acid, this hallucinogenic drug most commonly resembles a tab of paper.

Marijuana – An illegal drug. Also known as weed or pot; besides alcohol, marijuana is one of the most commonly-found drugs on campuses across the country.

Major – The focal point of a student's college studies; a specific topic that is studied for a degree. Examples of majors include physics, English, history, computer science, economics, business, and music. Many students decide on a specific major before arriving on campus, while others are simply "undecided" and figure it out later. Those who are extremely interested in two areas can also choose to double major.

Meal Block – The equivalent of one meal. Students on a "meal plan" usually receive a fixed number of meals per week.

Each meal, or "block," can be redeemed at the school's dining facilities in place of cash. More often than not, if a student fails to use their weekly allotment of meal blocks, they will be forfeited.

Minor – An additional focal point in a student's education. Often serving as a compliment or addition to a student's main area of focus, a minor has fewer requirements and prerequisites to fulfill than a major. Minors are not required for graduation from most schools; however some students who want to further explore many different interests choose to have both a major and a minor.

Mushrooms – An illegal drug. Also known as "shrooms," this drug looks like regular mushrooms but are extremely hallucinogenic.

Off-Campus Housing – Housing from a particular landlord or rental group that is not affiliated with the university. Depending on the college, off-campus housing can range from extremely popular to non-existent. Those students who choose to live off campus are typically given more freedom, but they also have to deal with things such as possible subletting scenarios, furniture, and bills. In addition to these factors, rental prices and distance often affect a student's decision to move off campus.

Office Hours – Time that teachers set aside for students who have questions about the coursework. Office hours are a good place for students to go over any problems and to show interest in the subject material.

Pledging – The time after a student has gone through rush, received a bid, and has chosen a particular fraternity or sorority they would like to join. Pledging usually lasts anywhere from one to two semesters. Once the pledging period is complete and a particular student has done everything that is required to become a member, they are considered a brother or sister. If a fraternity or a sorority would decide to "haze" a group of students, these initiation rituals would take place during the pledging period.

Private Institution – A school that does not use taxpayers dollars to help subsidize education costs. Private schools typically cost more than public schools and are usually smaller.

Prof – Slang for "professor."

Public Institution – A school that uses taxpayers dollars to help subsidize education costs. Public schools are often a good value for in-state residents and tend to be larger than most private colleges.

Quarter System (sometimes referred to as the Trimester System) – A type of academic calendar system. In this setup, students take classes for three academic periods. The first quarter usually starts in late September or early October and concludes right before Christmas. The second quarter usually starts around early to mid–January and finishes up around March or April. The last quarter, or "third quarter," usually starts in late March or early April and finishes up in late May or Mid-June. The fourth quarter is summer. The major difference between the quarter system and semester system is that students take more courses but with less coverage.

RA (Resident Assistant) – A student leader who is assigned to a particular floor in a dormitory in order to help to the other students who live there. A RA's duties include ensuring student safety and providing guidance or assistance wherever possible.

Recitation – An extension of a specific course; a "review" session of sorts. Because some classes are so large, recitations offer a setting with fewer students where students can ask questions and get help from professors or TAs in a more personalized environment. As a result, it is common for most large lecture classes to be supplemented with recitations.

Rolling Admissions – A form of admissions. Most commonly found at public institutions, schools with this type of policy continue to accept students throughout the year until their class sizes are met. For example, some schools begin accepting students as early as December and will continue to do so until April or May.

Room and Board – This is typically the combined cost of a university-owned room and a meal plan.

Room Draw/Housing Lottery – A common way to pick on-campus room assignments for the following year. If a student decides to remain in university-owned housing, they are assigned a unique number that, along with seniority, is used to choose their new rooms for the next year.

Rush – The period in which students can meet the brothers and sisters of a particular chapter and find out if a given fraternity or sorority is right for them. Rushing a fraternity or a sorority is not a requirement at any school. The goal of rush is to give students who are serious about pledging a feel for what to expect.

Semester System – The most common type of academic calendar system at college campuses. This setup typically includes two semesters in a given school year. The "fall" semester starts around the end of August or early September and finishes right before winter vacation. The "spring" semester usually starts in mid-January and ends around late April or May.

Student Center/Rec Center/Student Union – A common area on campus that often contains study areas, recreation facilities, and eateries. This building is often a good place to meet up with fellow students and is most commonly used as a hangout. Depending on the school, the student center can have a huge role or a non-existent role in campus life.

Student ID – A university-issued photo ID that serves as a student's key to many different functions within an institution. Some schools require students to show these cards in order to get into dorms, libraries, cafeterias, and other facilities. In addition to storing meal plan information, in some cases, a student ID can actually work as a debit card and allow students to purchase things from bookstores or local shops.

Suite – A type of dorm room. Unlike other places that have communal bathrooms that are shared by the entire floor, a suite has a private bathroom. Suite-style dorm rooms can house anywhere from two to ten students.

TA (Teacher's Assistant) – An undergraduate or grad student who helps in some manner with a specific course. In some cases, a TA will teach a class, assist a professor, grade assignments, or conduct office hours.

Undergraduate – A student who is in the process of studying for their Bachelor (college) degree.

ABOUT THE AUTHOR:

Despite the fact that I've only just finished my first year at Grinnell, I'm already madly in love with the place. When I was given the opportunity to write this guidebook, I was thrilled to have the chance to tell people who are trying to decide what their life is going to be like over the next four years about this little Iowan island in the sun, but I also wanted students to know about the things they should be prepared for that the college won't tell them. I hope I've managed to accomplish that in this guidebook. I apologize for any inaccuracies that I may have overlooked, or any significant details I left out, but as far as I know and have been able to find out, everything here is correct.

Right now, my major is undeclared, but I think that I will soon declare a double major in physics and history. My fuzzy vision of the future after Grinnell includes graduate school, trying to save the world, and after that....? First star to the right and straight on 'till morning, I suppose.

Lauren Standifer

LaurenStandifer@collegeprowler.com

Notes

Notes

Notes

Notes

Notes

Notes

Notes

Notes

Notes

Notes

Notes

Notes

Notes

Notes

Notes

Notes

Notes

Notes

Notes

Need More Help?

Do you have more questions about this school? Can't find a certain statistic? College Prowler is here to help. We are the best source of college information on the planet. We have a network of thousands of students who can get the latest information on any school to you ASAP. E-mail us at *info@collegeprowler.com* with your college-related questions. It's like having an older sibling show you the ropes!

Email Us Your College-Related Questions!

Check out **www.collegeprowler.com** for more details.
1.800.290.2682

Notes

Tell Us What Life Is Really Like At Your School!

Have you ever wanted to let people know what your school is really like? Now's your chance to help millions of high school students choose the right school.

Let your voice be heard and win cash and prizes!

Check out **www.collegeprowler.com** for more info!

Notes

Do You Have What It Takes To Get Admitted?

The College Prowler Road to College Counseling Program is here. An admissions officer will review your candidacy at the school of your choice and create a 12+ page personal admission plan. We rate your credentials with the same criteria used by school admissions committees. We assess your strengths and weaknesses and create a plan of action that makes a difference.

Check out **www.collegeprowler.com** or call 1.800.290.2682 for complete details.

Notes

Pros and Cons

Still can't figure out if this is the right school for you? You've already read through this in-depth guide; why not list the pros and cons? It will really help with narrowing down your decision and determining whether or not this school is right for you.

Pros	Cons

Notes

Need Help Paying For School?

Apply for our Scholarship!

College Prowler awards thousands of dollars a year to students who compose the best essays. E-mail *scholarship@collegeprowler.com* for more information, or call 1.800.290.2682.

Apply now at **www.collegeprowler.com**

Notes

Get Paid To Rep Your City!

Make money for college!

Earn cash by telling your friends about College Prowler!

Excellent Pay + Incentives + Bonuses

Compete with reps across the nation for cash bonuses

Gain marketing and communication skills

Build your resume and gain work experience for future career opportunities

Flexible work hours; make your own schedule

Opportunities for advancement

Contact sales@collegeprowler.com
Apply now at **www.collegeprowler.com**

Notes

Do You Own A Website?

Would you like to be an affiliate of one of the fastest-growing companies in the publishing industry? Our web affiliates generate a significant income based on customers whom they refer to our website. Start making some cash now! Contact *sales@collegeprowler.com* for more information or call 1.800.290.2682

Apply now at **www.collegeprowler.com**

Notes

Reach A Market Of Over 24 Million People.

Advertising with College Prowler will provide you with an environment in which your message will be read and respected. Place your message in a College Prowler guidebook, and let us start bringing long-lasting customers to you. We deliver high-quality ads in color or black-and-white throughout our guidebooks.

Contact Joey Rahimi
joey@collegeprowler.com
412.697.1391
1.800.290.2682

Check out **www.collegeprowler.com** for more info.

Notes

Write For Us!
Get Published! Voice Your Opinion.

Writing a College Prowler guidebook is both fun and rewarding; our open-ended format allows your own creativity free reign. Our writers have been featured in national newspapers and have seen their names in bookstores across the country. Now is your chance to break into the publishing industry with one of the country's fastest-growing publishers!

Apply now at **www.collegeprowler.com**

Contact *editor@collegeprowler.com* or call 1.800.290.2682 for more details.